Competition Policies for an Integrated World Economy

Integrating National Economies: Promise and Pitfalls

F. M. Scherer (Harvard University)
Competition Policies for an Integrated World Economy

Richard R. Nelson (Columbia University) and Sylvia Ostry (University of Toronto)
'High-Tech' Industrial Policies: Conflict and Cooperation

Alan O. Sykes (University of Chicago)
Product Standards for Internationally Integrated Goods Markets

Mitsuhiro Fukao (Bank of Japan)
Financial Integration, Corporate Governance, and the Performance of Multinational Companies

Richard J. Herring (University of Pennsylvania) and Robert E. Litan (Department of Justice/Brookings Institution)
Financial Regulation in a Global Economy

Ronald G. Ehrenberg (Cornell University)
Labor Markets and Integrating National Economies

Susan M. Collins (Brookings Institution/Georgetown University)
Distributive Issues: A Constraint on Global Integration

Robert Z. Lawrence (Harvard University)
Regionalism, Multilateralism, and Deeper Integration

Anne O. Krueger (Stanford University)
Trade Policies and Developing Nations

Richard N. Cooper (Harvard University)
Environment and Resource Policies for the World Economy

Ralph C. Bryant (Brookings Institution)
International Coordination of National Stabilization Policies

Vito Tanzi (International Monetary Fund)
Taxation in an Integrating World

Barry Eichengreen (University of California, Berkeley)
International Monetary Arrangements for the 21st Century

Miles Kahler (University of California, San Diego)
International Institutions and the Political Economy of Integration

Barry Bosworth (Brookings Institution) and Gur Ofer (Hebrew University)
Reforming Planned Economies in an Integrating World Economy

Robert L. Paarlberg (Wellesley College/Harvard University)
Leadership Abroad Begins at Home: U.S. Foreign Economic Policy after the Cold War

William Wallace (St. Antony's College, Oxford University)
Regional Integration: The West European Experience

Akihiko Tanaka (Institute of Oriental Culture, University of Tokyo)
The Politics of Deeper Integration: National Attitudes and Policies in Japan

Peter Rutland (Wesleyan University)
Russia, Eurasia, and the Global Economy

Susan L. Shirk (University of California, San Diego)
How China Opened Its Door: The Political Success of the PRC's Foreign Trade and Investment Reform

Stephan Haggard (University of California, San Diego)
Developing Nations and the Politics of Global Integration

F. M. Scherer

Competition Policies for an Integrated World Economy

THE BROOKINGS INSTITUTION
Washington, D.C.

Copyright © 1994
THE BROOKINGS INSTITUTION
1775 Massachusetts Avenue, N. W., Washington, D.C. 20036

Library of Congress Cataloging-in-Publication data:
Scherer, F. M. (Frederic M.)
Competition policies for an integrated world economy/F. M. Scherer.
p. cm. — (Integrating national economies)
Includes bibliographical references and index.
ISBN 0-8157-7798-1 — ISBN 0-8157-7797-3 (pbk.)
1. Commercial policy. 2. Competition, International.
3. International economic integration. I. Title. II. Series.
HF1412.S3 1994
337—dc20   94-11819
                                                          CIP

9 8 7 6 5 4 3 2 1

The paper used in this publication meets the minimum requirements of the
American National Standard for Information Sciences—Permanence of Paper
for Printed Library Materials, ANSI Z39.48-1984

Typeset in Plantin

Composition by Princeton Editorial Associates
Princeton, New Jersey

Printed by R. R. Donnelley and Sons Co.
Harrisonburg, Virginia

Foreword

*I*N the late 1940s, twenty-three nations ratified the first General Agreement on Tariffs and Trade. Since then, tariff barriers and quotas have been progressively reduced throughout much of the industrialized world, resulting in greatly expanded international trade. The Uruguay Round negotiations, concluded in December 1993, extended GATT's reach to agriculture, services, and intellectual property and clarified policies toward other aspects of trade. The question now arises, what steps remain to carry international economic integration beyond the impressive accomplishments already attained?

In this book, F. M. Scherer analyzes the three-way integration among international trade policies (as they emerged through the various GATT rounds), the competition policies nations and trading blocs implement to channel producers' behavior in procompetitive directions, and the strategies nations and individual enterprises pursue to enhance their trading advantage in the international marketplace. The author traces the intellectual foundations and subsequent evolution of these three policy domains, investigating closely the points at which they come into conflict. The book concludes with a proposal for new international competition policy instruments to curb avoidable restraints on competition while infringing minimally on national sovereignty.

F. M. Scherer is professor of business and government at the John F. Kennedy School of Government, Harvard University. He is grateful to Robert Lawrence, Alexis Jacquemin, Jiro Tamura, Erich Kaufer, Raymond Vernon, Frederic Jenny, Yves Bourdet, Yoichi Nemoto, the participants in a Brookings review conference on October 15, 1993, and the participants in the Harvard Law School seminar on Law and Economics for their constructive criticisms and suggestions. Erich Kaufer, Eleanor Fox, and Sigmund Timberg contributed hard-to-find materials used in preparing the manuscript. The author also received valuable assistance from the reference librarians at the John F. Kennedy School and the Harvard Law School.

Tal Gurion provided research assistance at several stages in the project. Caroline Lalire edited the manuscript, and David Bearce verified its factual content. Maureen Schake nursed successive versions of the manuscript through word processing, with final editing incorporated by David Rossetti. Princeton Editorial Associates prepared the index.

Funding for the project came from the Center for Global Partnership of the Japan Foundation, the Curry Fund, the Ford Foundation, the Korea Foundation, the Tokyo Club Foundation for Global Studies, the United States–Japan Foundation, and the Alex C. Walker Educational and Charitable Foundation. The author and Brookings are grateful for their support.

The views expressed in this book are those of the author and should not be ascribed to any of the persons or organizations acknowledged above, or to the trustees, officers, or staff members of the Brookings Institution.

BRUCE K. MACLAURY
President

June 1994
Washington, D.C.

Contents

Figures

Preface to the Studies on Integrating National Economies

*E*CONOMIC interdependence among nations has increased sharply in the past half century. For example, while the value of total production of industrial countries increased at a rate of about 9 percent a year on average between 1964 and 1992, the value of the exports of those nations grew at an average rate of 12 percent, and lending and borrowing across national borders through banks surged upward even more rapidly at 23 percent a year. This international economic interdependence has contributed to significantly improved standards of living for most countries. Continuing international economic integration holds out the promise of further benefits. Yet the increasing sensitivity of national economies to events and policies originating abroad creates dilemmas and pitfalls if national policies and international cooperation are poorly managed.

The Brookings Project on Integrating National Economies, of which this study is a component, focuses on the interplay between two fundamental facts about the world at the end of the twentieth century. First, the world will continue for the foreseeable future to be organized politically into nation-states with sovereign governments. Second, increasing economic integration among nations will continue to erode differences among national economies and undermine the autonomy of national governments. The project explores the opportunities and tensions arising from these two facts.

Scholars from a variety of disciplines have produced twenty-one studies for the first phase of the project. Each study examines the heightened competition between national political sovereignty and increased cross-border economic integration. This preface identifies background themes and issues common to all the studies and provides a brief overview of the project as a whole.[1]

---

1. A complete list of authors and study titles is included at the beginning of this volume, facing the title page.

Increasing World Economic Integration

Two underlying sets of causes have led nations to become more closely intertwined. First, technological, social, and cultural changes have sharply reduced the effective economic distances among nations. Second, many of the government policies that traditionally inhibited cross-border transactions have been relaxed or even dismantled.

The same improvements in transportation and communications technology that make it much easier and cheaper for companies in New York to ship goods to California, for residents of Strasbourg to visit relatives in Marseilles, and for investors in Hokkaido to buy and sell shares on the Tokyo Stock Exchange facilitate trade, migration, and capital movements spanning nations and continents. The sharply reduced costs of moving goods, money, people, and information underlie the profound economic truth that technology has made the world markedly smaller.

New communications technology has been especially significant for financial activity. Computers, switching devices, and telecommunications satellites have slashed the cost of transmitting information internationally, of confirming transactions, and of paying for transactions. In the 1950s, for example, foreign exchange could be bought and sold only during conventional business hours in the initiating party's time zone. Such transactions can now be carried out instantaneously twenty-four hours a day. Large banks pass the management of their worldwide foreign-exchange positions around the globe from one branch to another, staying continuously ahead of the setting sun.

Such technological innovations have increased the knowledge of potentially profitable international exchanges and of economic opportunities abroad. Those developments, in turn, have changed consumers' and producers' tastes. Foreign goods, foreign vacations, foreign financial investments—virtually anything from other nations—have lost some of their exotic character.

Although technological change permits increased contact among nations, it would not have produced such dramatic effects if it had been countermanded by government policies. Governments have traditionally taxed goods moving in international trade, directly restricted imports and subsidized exports, and tried to limit international capital movements. Those policies erected "separation fences" at the borders of nations. From the perspective of private sector agents, separation fences imposed extra costs on cross-border transactions. They reduced trade and, in some cases, eliminated it. During the 1930s governments used such policies with particular zeal, a practice now believed to have deepened and lengthened the Great Depression.

After World War II, most national governments began—sometimes unilaterally, more often collaboratively—to lower their separation fences, to make them more permeable, or sometimes even to tear down parts of them. The multilateral negotiations under the auspices of the General Agreement on Trade and Tariffs (GATT)—for example, the Kennedy Round in the 1960s, the Tokyo Round in the 1970s, and most recently the protracted negotiations of the Uruguay Round, formally signed only in April 1994—stand out as the most prominent examples of fence lowering for trade in goods. Though contentious and marked by many compromises, the GATT negotiations are responsible for sharp reductions in at-the-border restrictions on trade in goods and services. After the mid-1980s a large number of developing countries moved unilaterally to reduce border barriers and to pursue outwardly oriented policies.

The lowering of fences for financial transactions began later and was less dramatic. Nonetheless, by the 1990s government restrictions on capital flows, especially among the industrial countries, were much less important and widespread than at the end of World War II and in the 1950s.

By shrinking the economic distances among nations, changes in technology would have progressively integrated the world economy even in the absence of reductions in governments' separation fences. Reductions in separation fences would have enhanced interdependence even without the technological innovations. Together, these two sets of evolutionary changes have reinforced each other and strikingly transformed the world economy.

Changes in the Government of Nations

Simultaneously with the transformation of the global economy, major changes have occurred in the world's political structure. First, the number of governmental decisionmaking units in the world has expanded markedly and political power has been diffused more broadly among them. Rising nationalism and, in some areas, heightened ethnic tensions have accompanied that increasing political pluralism.

The history of membership in international organizations documents the sharp growth in the number of independent states. For example, only 44 nations participated in the Bretton Woods conference of July 1944, which gave birth to the International Monetary Fund. But by the end of 1970, the IMF had 118 member nations. The number of members grew to 150 by the mid-1980s and to 178 by December 1993. Much of this growth reflects the collapse of colonial empires. Although many nations today are small and carry little individual weight in the global economy, their combined influence is considerable and their interests cannot be ignored as easily as they were in the past.

A second political trend, less visible but equally important, has been the gradual loss of the political and economic hegemony of the United States. Immediately after World War II, the United States by itself accounted for more than one-third of world production. By the early 1990s the U.S. share had fallen to about one-fifth. Concurrently, the political and economic influence of the European colonial powers continued to wane, and the economic significance of nations outside Europe and North America, such as Japan, Korea, Indonesia, China, Brazil, and Mexico, increased. A world in which economic power and influence are widely diffused has displaced a world in which one or a few nations effectively dominated international decisionmaking.

Turmoil and the prospect of fundamental change in the formerly centrally planned economies compose a third factor causing radical changes in world politics. During the era of central planning, governments in those nations tried to limit external influences on their economies. Now leaders in the formerly planned economies are trying to adopt reforms modeled on Western capitalist principles. To the extent that these efforts succeed, those nations will increase their economic involvement with the rest of the world. Political and economic alignments among the Western industrialized nations will be forced to adapt.

Governments and scholars have begun to assess these three trends, but their far-reaching ramifications will not be clear for decades.

Dilemmas for National Policies

Cross-border economic integration and national political sovereignty have increasingly come into conflict, leading to a growing mismatch between the economic and political structures of the world. The effective domains of economic markets have come to coincide less and less with national governmental jurisdictions.

When the separation fences at nations' borders were high, governments and citizens could sharply distinguish "international" from "domestic" policies. International policies dealt with at-the-border barriers, such as tariffs and quotas, or responded to events occurring abroad. In contrast, domestic policies were concerned with everything behind the nation's borders, such as competition and antitrust rules, corporate governance, product standards, worker safety, regulation and supervision of financial institutions, environmental protection, tax codes, and the government's budget. Domestic policies were regarded as matters about which nations were sovereign, to be determined by the preferences of the nation's citizens and its political institutions, without regard for effects on other nations.

As separation fences have been lowered and technological innovations have shrunk economic distances, a multitude of formerly neglected differences among nations' domestic policies have become exposed to international scrutiny. National governments and international negotiations must thus increasingly deal with "deeper"—behind-the-border—integration. For example, if country A permits companies to emit air and water pollutants whereas country B does not, companies that use pollution-generating methods of production will find it cheaper to produce in country A. Companies in country B that compete internationally with companies in country A are likely to complain that foreign competitors enjoy unfair advantages and to press for international pollution standards.

Deeper integration requires analysis of the economic and the political aspects of virtually all nonborder policies and practices. Such issues have already figured prominently in negotiations over the evolution of the European Community, over the Uruguay Round of GATT negotiations, over the North American Free Trade Agreement (NAFTA), and over the bilateral economic relationships between Japan and the United States. Future debates about behind-the-border policies will occur with increasing frequency and prove at least as complex and contentious as the past negotiations regarding at-the-border restrictions.

Tensions about deeper integration arise from three broad sources: cross-border spillovers, diminished national autonomy, and challenges to political sovereignty.

Cross-Border Spillovers

Some activities in one nation produce consequences that spill across borders and affect other nations. Illustrations of these spillovers abound. Given the impact of modern technology of banking and securities markets in creating interconnected networks, lax rules in one nation erode the ability of all other nations to enforce banking and securities rules and to deal with fraudulent transactions. Given the rapid diffusion of knowledge, science and technology policies in one nation generate knowledge that other nations can use without full payment. Labor market policies become matters of concern to other nations because workers migrate in search of work; policies in one nation can trigger migration that floods or starves labor markets elsewhere. When one nation dumps pollutants into the air or water that other nations breathe or drink, the matter goes beyond the unitary concern of the polluting nation and becomes a matter for international negotiation. Indeed, the hydrocarbons that are emitted into the atmosphere when individual nations burn coal for generating electricity contribute to global warming and are thereby a matter of concern for the entire world.

The tensions associated with cross-border spillovers can be especially vexing when national policies generate outcomes alleged to be competitively inequitable, as in the example in which country A permits companies to emit pollutants and country B does not. Or consider a situation in which country C requires commodities, whether produced at home or abroad, to meet certain design standards, justified for safety reasons. Foreign competitors may find it too expensive to meet these standards. In that event, the standards in C act very much like tariffs or quotas, effectively narrowing or even eliminating foreign competition for domestic producers. Citing examples of this sort, producers or governments in individual nations often complain that business is not conducted on a "level playing field." Typically, the complaining nation proposes that *other* nations adjust their policies to moderate or remove the competitive inequities.

Arguments for creating a level playing field are troublesome at best. International trade occurs precisely because of differences among nations—in resource endowments, labor skills, and consumer tastes. Nations specialize in producing goods and services in which they are relatively most efficient. In a fundamental sense, cross-border trade is valuable because the playing field is *not* level.

When David Ricardo first developed the theory of comparative advantage, he focused on differences among nations owing to climate or technology. But Ricardo could as easily have ascribed the productive differences to differing "social climates" as to physical or technological climates. Taking all "climatic" differences as given, the theory of comparative advantage argues that free trade among nations will maximize global welfare.

Taken to its logical extreme, the notion of leveling the playing field implies that nations should become homogeneous in all major respects. But that recommendation is unrealistic and even pernicious. Suppose country A decides that it is too poor to afford the costs of a clean environment, and will thus permit the production of goods that pollute local air and water supplies. Or suppose it concludes that it cannot afford stringent protections for worker safety. Country A will then argue that it is inappropriate for other nations to impute to country A the value they themselves place on a clean environment and safety standards (just as it would be inappropriate to impute the A valuations to the environment of other nations). The core of the idea of political sovereignty is to permit national residents to order their lives and property in accord with their own preferences.

Which perspective about differences among nations in behind-the-border policies is more compelling? Is country A merely exercising its national preferences and appropriately exploiting its comparative advantage in goods that are dirty or dangerous to produce? Or does a legitimate international problem exist that justifies pressure from other nations urging country A to accept changes in its policies (thus curbing its national sovereignty)? When national governments negotiate resolutions to such questions—trying to agree whether individual nations are legitimately exercising sovereign choices or, alternatively, engaging in behavior that is unfair or damaging to other nations—the dialogue is invariably contentious because the resolutions depend on the typically complex circumstances of the international spillovers and on the relative weights accorded to the interests of particular individuals and particular nations.

Diminished National Autonomy

As cross-border economic integration increases, governments experience greater difficulties in trying to control events within their borders. Those difficulties, summarized by the term *diminished autonomy*, are the second set of reasons why tensions arise from the competition between political sovereignty and economic integration.

For example, nations adjust monetary and fiscal policies to influence domestic inflation and employment. In setting these policies, smaller countries have always been somewhat constrained by foreign economic events and policies. Today, however, all nations are constrained, often severely. More than in the past, therefore, nations may be better able to achieve their economic goals if they work together collaboratively in adjusting their macroeconomic policies.

Diminished autonomy and cross-border spillovers can sometimes be allowed to persist without explicit international cooperation to deal with them. States in the United States adopt their own tax systems and set policies for assistance to poor single people without any formal cooperation or limitation. Market pressures operate to force a degree of de facto cooperation. If one state taxes corporations too heavily, it knows business will move elsewhere. (Those familiar with older debates about "fiscal federalism" within the United States and other nations will recognize the similarity between those issues and the emerging international debates about deeper integration of national economies.) Analogously, differences among nations in regulations, standards, policies, institutions, and even social and cultural preferences create economic incentives for a kind of arbitrage that erodes or eliminates the differences. Such pressures involve not only the conventional arbitrage that exploits price differentials (buying at one point in geographic space or time and selling at another) but also shifts in the location of production facilities and in the residence of factors of production.

In many other cases, however, cross-border spillovers, arbitrage pressures, and diminished effectiveness of national policies can produce unwanted consequences. In cases involving what economists call externalities (external economies and diseconomies), national governments may need to cooperate to promote mutual interests. For example, population growth, continued urbanization, and the more intensive exploitation of natural resources generate external diseconomies not only within but across national boundaries. External economies generated when benefits spill across national jurisdictions probably also increase in importance (for instance, the gains from basic research and from control of communicable diseases).

None of these situations is new, but technological change and the reduction of tariffs and quotas heighten their importance. When one nation produces goods (such as scientific research) or "bads" (such as pollution) that significantly affect other nations, individual governments acting sequentially and noncooperatively cannot deal effectively with the resulting issues. In the absence of explicit cooperation and political leadership, too few collective goods and too many collective bads will be supplied.

Challenges to Political Sovereignty

The pressures from cross-border economic integration sometimes even lead individuals or governments to challenge the core assumptions of national political sovereignty. Such challenges are a third source of tensions about deeper integration.

The existing world system of nation-states assumes that a nation's residents are free to follow their own values and to select their own political arrangements without interference from others. Similarly, property rights are allocated by nation. (The so-called global commons, such as outer space and the deep seabed, are the sole exceptions.) A nation is assumed to have the sovereign right to exploit its property in accordance with its own preferences and policies. Political sovereignty is thus analogous to the concept of consumer sovereignty (the presumption that the individual consumer best knows his or her own interests and should exercise them freely).

In times of war, some nations have had sovereignty wrested from them by force. In earlier eras, a handful of individuals or groups have questioned the premises of political sovereignty. With the profound increases in economic integration in recent decades, however, a larger number of individuals and groups—and occasionally even their national governments—have identified circumstances in which, it is claimed, some universal or international set of values should take precedence over the preferences or policies of particular nations.

Some groups seize on human-rights issues, for example, or what they deem to be egregiously inappropriate political arrangements in other nations. An especially prominent case occurred when citizens in many nations labeled the former apartheid policies of South Africa an affront to universal values and emphasized that the South African government was not legitimately representing the interests of a majority of South Africa's residents. Such views caused many national governments to apply economic sanctions against South Africa. Examples of value conflicts are not restricted to human rights, however. Groups focusing on environmental issues characterize tropical rain forests as the lungs of the world and the genetic repository for numerous species of plants and animals that are the heritage of all mankind. Such views lead Europeans, North Americans, or Japanese to challenge the timber-cutting policies of Brazilians and Indonesians. A recent controversy over tuna fishing with long drift nets that kill porpoises is yet another example. Environmentalists in the United States whose sensibilities were offended by the drowning of porpoises required U.S. boats at some additional expense to amend their fishing practices. The U.S. fishermen, complaining about imported tuna caught with less regard for porpoises, persuaded the U.S. government to ban such tuna imports (both direct imports from the countries in which the tuna is caught and indirect imports shipped via third countries). Mexico and Venezuela were the main countries affected by this ban; a GATT dispute panel sided with Mexico against the United States in the controversy, which further upset the U.S. environmental community.

A common feature of all such examples is the existence, real or alleged, of "psychological externalities" or "political failures." Those holding such views reject untrammeled political sovereignty for nation-states in deference to universal or non-national values. They wish to constrain the exercise of individual nations' sovereignties through international negotiations or, if necessary, by even stronger intervention.

The Management of International Convergence

In areas in which arbitrage pressures and cross-border spillovers are weak and psychological or political externalities are largely absent, national governments may encounter few problems with deeper integration. Diversity across nations may persist quite easily. But at the other extreme, arbitrage and spillovers in some areas may be so strong that they threaten to erode national diversity completely. Or psychological and political sensitivities may be asserted too powerfully to be ignored. Governments will then be confronted with serious tensions, and national policies and behaviors may eventually converge to common, worldwide patterns (for example, subject to internationally agreed norms or minimum standards). Eventual convergence across nations, if it occurs, could happen in a harmful way (national policies and practices being driven to a least common denominator with externalities ignored, in effect a "race to the bottom") or it could occur with mutually beneficial results ("survival of the fittest and the best").

Each study in this series addresses basic questions about the management of international convergence: if, when, and how national governments should intervene to try to influence the consequences of arbitrage pressures, cross-border spillovers, diminished autonomy, and the assertion of psychological or political externalities. A wide variety of responses is conceivable. We identify six, which should be regarded not as distinct categories but as ranges along a continuum.

National autonomy defines a situation at one end of the continuum in which national governments make decentralized decisions with little or no consultation and no explicit cooperation. This response represents political sovereignty at its strongest, undiluted by any international management of convergence.

Mutual recognition, like national autonomy, presumes decentralized decisions by national governments and relies on market competition to guide the process of international convergence. Mutual recognition, however, entails exchanges of information and consultations among governments to constrain the formation of national regulations and policies. As understood in discussions of economic integration within the European Community, moreover, mutual recognition entails an explicit acceptance by each member nation of the regulations, standards, and certification procedures of other members. For example, mutual recognition allows wine or liquor produced in any European Union country to be sold in all twelve member countries even if production standards in member countries differ. Doctors licensed in France are permitted to practice in Germany, and vice versa, even if licensing procedures in the two countries differ.

Governments may agree on rules that restrict their freedom to set policy or that promote gradual convergence in the structure of policy. As international consultations and monitoring of compliance with such rules become more important, this situation can be described as *monitored decentralization*. The Group of Seven finance ministers meetings, supplemented by the IMF's surveillance over exchange rate and macroeconomic policies, illustrate this approach to management.

Coordination goes further than mutual recognition and monitored decentralization in acknowledging convergence pressures. It is also more ambitious in promoting intergovernmental cooperation to deal with them. Coordination involves jointly designed mutual adjustments of national policies. In clear-cut cases of coordination, bargaining occurs and governments agree to behave differently from the ways they would have behaved without the agreement. Examples include the World Health Organization's procedures for controlling communicable diseases and the 1987 Montreal Protocol (to a 1985 framework convention) for the protection of stratospheric ozone by reducing emissions of chlorofluorocarbons.

Explicit harmonization, which requires still higher levels of intergovernmental cooperation, may require agreement on regional standards or world standards. Explicit harmonization typically entails still greater departures from decentralization in decisionmaking and still further strengthening of international institutions. The 1988 agreement among major central banks to set minimum standards for the required capital positions of commercial banks (reached through the Committee on Banking Regulations and Supervisory Practices at the Bank for International Settlements) is an example of partially harmonized regulations.

At the opposite end of the spectrum from national autonomy lies *federalist mutual governance,* which implies continuous bargaining and joint, centralized decisionmaking. To make federalist mutual governance work would require greatly strengthened supranational institutions. This end of the management spectrum, now relevant only as an analytical benchmark, is a possible outcome that can be imagined for the middle or late decades of the twenty-first century, possibly even sooner for regional groupings like the European Union.

Overview of the Brookings Project

Despite their growing importance, the issues of deeper economic integration and its competition with national political sovereignty were largely neglected in the 1980s. In 1992 the Brookings Institution initiated its project on Integrating National Economies to direct attention to these important questions.

In studying this topic, Brookings sought and received the cooperation of some of the world's leading economists, political scientists, foreign-policy specialists, and government officials, representing all regions of the world. Although some functional areas require a special focus on European, Japanese, and North American perspectives, at all junctures the goal was to include, in addition, the perspectives of developing nations and the formerly centrally planned economies.

The first phase of the project commissioned the twenty-one scholarly studies listed at the beginning of the book. One or two lead discussants, typically residents of parts of the world other than the area where the author resides, were asked to comment on each study.

Authors enjoyed substantial freedom to design their individual studies, taking due account of the overall themes and goals of the project. The guidelines for the studies requested that at least some of the analysis be carried out with a non-normative perspective. In effect, authors were asked to develop a "baseline" of what might happen in the absence of changed policies or further international cooperation. For their normative analyses, authors were asked to start with an agnostic posture that did not prejudge the net benefits or costs resulting from integration. The project organizers themselves had no presumption about whether national diversity is better or worse than international convergence or about what the individual studies should conclude regarding the desirability of increased integration. On the contrary, each author was asked to address the trade-offs in his or her issue area between diversity and convergence and to locate the area, currently and prospectively, on the spectrum of international management possibilities running between national autonomy through mutual recognition to coordination and explicit harmonization.

HENRY J. AARON   SUSAN M. COLLINS

RALPH C. BRYANT   ROBERT Z. LAWRENCE

Chapter I

Introduction

"A NTITRUST"—the assortment of policies pursued with intermittent fervor in the United States since 1890 to foster competitive market processes—has a disagreeably negative ring. Our European cousins have accentuated the positive by choosing "competition policy" to characterize their corresponding rules of the road. However one resolves the semantic problem, such rules have been accorded an increasingly prominent role in industrialized nations' policy portfolios during the second half of the twentieth century.

This book explores the three-way interface between competition policy, the strategies individual nations and their national champions pursue toward transactions that span national boundaries (that is, national trading and investment strategies), and the policies groups of nations adopt to harmonize their trading relationships (that is, international trade policies).

The Policy Goals

Superficially, competition policy and international trade policy have much in common, especially in their basic objectives. Thus the preamble to the 1947 General Agreement on Tariffs and Trade (GATT), the Magna Carta of international trading relations, articulates as goals:

> raising standards of living, ensuring full employment and a large and steadily growing volume of real income and effective demand, developing the full use of the resources of the world and expanding the production and exchange of goods;

and as instruments toward achieving those goals:

the substantial reduction of tariffs and other barriers to trade and the elimination of discriminatory treatment in international commerce.[1]

Competition policy seeks to remove restraints upon and barriers to competitive transacting, usually (although not necessarily) within a specific national market. It attempts thereby to facilitate the efficient allocation of economic resources. The ultimate result, as Adam Smith proclaimed in a passage extolling the benefits of competition within nations and free trade among nations, is to "render the annual revenue of the society as great as [possible]," that is, to maximize real income.[2]

These are ideals. From them, deviations can intrude, and policy conflicts can arise. Nations that have accepted the various GATT principles often evade them in practice by erecting nontariff barriers to trade. Sellers engage in brinkmanship against competition policy rules. The policies themselves can be administered clumsily, missing their intended mark, or they may be subverted to protect *competitors,* rather than encouraging *competition* per se.[3] Jurisdictional complexities abound when business firms' activities encompass multiple nations. The Gillette Company's acquisition of Wilkinson Sword, to cite the most extreme example, had to be cleared by fourteen distinct merger review offices.[4] Intricate legal conflicts arise when the competition policy authority of one nation attempts to exercise "extraterritorial jurisdiction," regulating anticompetitive practices of foreign companies that spill over—for example, through exports—onto the acting authority's home turf.

At their best, competition policy and international trade policy reinforce each other and facilitate the attainment of their mutual goals. At worst, they depart from their stated goals and interfere with each other's ability to sustain positive outcomes.

The Task at Hand

This book surveys the domains of policy conflict, complementarity, and substitutability. The remainder of this chapter pins down more precisely the goal structures of international trade policy and competition policy, sketching a theoretical framework for understanding how

1. "General Agreement on Tariffs and Trade," signed at Geneva October 30, 1947, (1947, p. 7).

2. Smith ([1776] 1937, bk. 4, chap. 2, p. 423).

3. For a collection that emphasizes this pessimistic view, see Mackay, Miller, and Yandle (1987).

4. See "OECD Committee Lacks Enthusiasm for Draft International Antitrust Code," *Antitrust and Trade Regulation Report,* December 16, 1993, p. 771.

they can conflict. Chapter 2 surveys the evolution over two centuries of national trading and investment policies and the attempts to harmonize them through multilateral trading agreements. Chapter 3 provides a parallel survey of emerging national and international competition policies. Chapter 4 is the book's substantive core, undertaking a thorough analysis of the main challenges confronting competition policy at its interface with international trade policy. Examined in turn are various kinds of cartels, market dominance, trade-affecting vertical restraints, price discrimination and its treatment under competition policy and trade policy, and the special problems posed by boundary-hurdling multinational corporations. Chapter 5 recommends substantive and procedural improvements at the two policy domains' intersection.

Theory Underlying the Policy Goals

Efforts to reduce barriers to international trade begin from the premise that free and open trade provides collective benefits to the citizens of trading nations. Through trade each nation can specialize in producing, both for use at home and export, the goods in whose supply its business enterprises have comparative advantage, that is, for which they have relatively low supply costs. In this way the world's goods and services are provided most efficiently, which means that the maximum amount of output is realized from finite resources. Efficiency results from using specialized resources to best advantage; from affording each nation's consumers a wide variety of goods and services among which they can choose; from concentrating the production of any given product within sufficiently few sources to ensure that design, production, and marketing economies of scale are exploited as fully as they can be; and from ensuring that, despite this concentration, sufficiently many supply sources remain to maintain tough competitive pressure on each individual supplier. From vigorous competition flow, in turn, pricing that sends the right signals to market participants, fostering efficient resource allocation; pressure forcing suppliers to manage their operations tightly, that is, at minimum unit cost; and incentives to introduce superior new products and production processes, because only through innovation can a firm outrace its peers and realize supra-competitive profits.

The difficulty with this utopian scenario is that individual nations and their national champion industries have incentives to deviate from free trade to aggrandize their narrow interests.[5] By adeptly raising import and

---

5. For recent analyses of these tendencies under the rubric "strategic trade policy," see Krugman (1986); Krugman (1990); and Lawrence and Schultze (1990).

Figure 1-1. *International Trade Policy Payoff Matrix*

		Nation B's strategy choices	
		Maintain open markets	Erect trade barriers
Nation A's	Maintain open markets	2,2	4,1
strategy choices	Erect trade barriers	1,4	3,3

export tariffs, one trading partner can alter price relationships to its own advantage, and rents (analogous to monopoly profits) can be captured from the other partner. The terms of trade can also be manipulated profitably by conferring monopoly power on the home nation's exporting firms and protecting them from import competition through trade barriers. Comparative cost positions can be shifted, and the terms of trade can be modified, by subsidizing national champions' efforts to achieve technological innovations and by shielding such enterprises from import competition. The object is to help them exploit economies of scale more fully and sell their products at monopoly prices.[6] And at the macroeconomic level, when appreciable unemployment exists, one nation may attempt to win jobs away from its trading partners by exporting vigorously to them while erecting barriers to imports that threaten its own industries.

Such trade-manipulating strategies can be profitable if implemented unilaterally while other nations practice free trade. But if all nations play the strategic trading game, or if others retaliate with countermeasures against some nation's strategizing, the gains from unilateral deviation vanish, and all are likely to be worse off than they would have been if they had adhered to free trade rules.

In this respect, trading relations among nations and their national champions provide an example of the classic Prisoner's Dilemma game, with a payoff matrix (for two representative nations, A and B) illustrated in figure 1-1.[7] Each nation is assumed to face a simplified strategy choice dichotomy: openness or the erection of trade barriers. The payoffs to the nations' citizens, ranked from 1 (best) to 4 (worst), depend upon the

6. As Alfred Marshall lamented, "In the eighteenth century . . . England had something approaching to a monopoly of the new methods of manufacture; and each bale of her goods would be sold—at all events when their supply was artificially limited—in return for a vast amount of the produce of foreign countries. . . . [But] her improvements have been followed, and latterly often anticipated, by America and Germany and other countries: and her special products have lost nearly all their monopoly value." Marshall (1961, vol. 1, pp. 672–73).

7. Classic explications include Schelling (1960); and Shubik (1982).

nations' strategy choices. In the payoff matrix of figure 1-1, nation A's payoff is listed before the commas, nation B's after the commas. The highest payoff for nation A comes when A erects trade barriers while B opens its markets for free trade. The worst payoff for A comes from free trading while others erect barriers. Under classic game-theoretic reasoning, nation A asks what its best payoff will be if B practices openness. The answer is, the erection of trade barriers (that is, with a payoff of 1, compared with 2 if A also practices openness). If B erects barriers, the preferred choice for A is also to erect barriers. Thus, whichever strategy choice B makes, the erection of barriers yields the higher payoff to A. In the language of game theory, erecting barriers is a "dominant solution." If nation B reasons symmetrically, it too will erect trade barriers, and the game will attain its "noncooperative solution," with each nation erecting barriers, realizing payoffs of 3, 3. But the noncooperative solution is a mutually disadvantageous solution. If nations A and B could find some way to cooperate in maintaining open markets, both could do better, with higher-ranked payoffs of 2, 2, than they would by reciprocally erecting trade barriers. Formal game theory analyzes how threats and inducements, and dynamically, how the fear of retaliation and counter-retaliation, can help parties surmount the Prisoner's Dilemma and attain cooperative win-win solutions.

The various GATT negotiating rounds have at bottom been an exercise in solving the Prisoner's Dilemmas of international trading relations. Nations have agreed to move away from trade-barring choices, at least in the realm of tariffs, and toward mutually rewarding market openness. Considering the temptations to depart from free trade (that is, the hope of achieving a "1" payoff), the GATT experience has been a remarkable success. But that success is attended by continuing danger. One of the measures that nations use to induce their peers' compliance with the agreed-upon free trade rules (and sometimes with those that have not been agreed upon) is the threat to retaliate against trading partners' injury-causing subsidies or discrimination by selectively imposing countervailing barriers, such as elevated tariffs. Threatening to erect trade barriers in retaliation against actual or perceived trade rule violations is analogous to threatening war as a deterrent to military aggression, but with less deadly consequences, and hence less reluctance on the part of nations to engage in brinkmanship. Thus arises the genuine danger that "we had to destroy free trade in order to save it."

When violations do occur, and especially when trade is distorted because exports are subsidized or "dumped," their impact is usually felt first and most directly by specific industries in the nation contemplating retaliatory restrictions. The enforcement mechanisms under GATT and

Figure 1-2. *Profit Matrix for Interfirm Rivalry*

Company B's strategy choices

		Collude	Chisel
Company A's	Collude	2,2	4,1
strategy choices	Chisel	1,4	3,3

national implementations thereof tend, therefore, to focus on protecting particular industries from material injury, not the mass of consumers for whose benefit the global free trading consensus is intended to function. This focus on protecting specific industries poses potentially serious problems of goal confusion. Legislators and bureaucrats may lose sight of the ultimate intended beneficiaries of trade policy in their instrumental concern with enforcing the rules, or when the lobbying efforts of well-organized industrial interests overwhelm concern for politically impotent consumers. This is a chronic problem to which I return later.

Like international trade policy, competition policy seeks to secure for consumers the benefits of free and open competition. To serve that purpose, competition policy bureaucrats focus, like trade policy enforcers, on conditions in particular industries. But they bring to bear a radically different instrumental viewpoint. The reason for an active competition policy is the fear that, absent appropriate government intervention, individual firms within an industry will behave in ways that harm consumers and subvert economic efficiency.

In essence, competition policy enforcers recognize that firms, like nations, find themselves in Prisoner's Dilemma situations. The standard case is represented in figure 1-2. It assumes that a particular product is supplied by two sellers, A and B. To oversimplify for theoretical clarity, each seller faces two strategy choices in implementing its pricing policy: it can set collusively high prices, or it can "chisel" by quoting a low price that undercuts the joint monopoly profit-maximizing value. As in the international trade policy matrix, payoffs are specified only ordinally, with the most profitable outcome for a given firm having the value 1 and the least profitable outcome a value of 4. Considering the situation from company A's perspective, a higher profit comes from chiseling if company B sets a high collusive price. If company B chisels, company A will fare poorly indeed if it sets a high price and loses most of its customers; its better payoff comes from chiseling too. Chiseling is a dominant strategy for company A. If company B reasons symmetrically, it will also chisel. But if both chisel, they will divide the market at low prices and realize the relatively unfavorable payoffs 3, 3. Both could be better off, and perhaps much better off, if they can find a way of cooperating to sustain high collusive prices and share a more lucrative market yielding payoffs 2, 2. A vast literature explores how real-world firms avoid the Prisoner's Dilemma and realize high-price, high-profit cooperative solutions.[8] The methods include merger to consolidate a monopoly position, binding cartel agreements, less formal collusive arrangements, price leadership, threat and counterthreat strategies, and much else.

By the logic of their mandate, competition policy enforcers work to *prevent* firms under their jurisdiction from solving the pricing game cooperatively. They are (or should be) concerned with enhancing the welfare of consumers, not with maximizing producer profits. If some complications that will intrude at diverse points in later chapters are ignored, consumer welfare is higher when producers set prices competitively than when pricing is cooperative or collusive. This occurs because monopoly prices transfer purchasing power from consumers to producers, because monopoly pricing inefficiently distorts the allocation of resources, and because a high-price position may permit producers to become fat, wasteful, and unprogressive.[9] Competition policy agencies encourage competitive outcomes by keeping markets competitively structured, for example, by breaking up monopolistic consolidations and preventing monopoly-enhancing mergers; by establishing rules of the game favoring competitive conduct, such as prohibiting cartels and punishing collusion; and (more controversially) by directly constraining through regulation the prices monopolistic enterprises can charge.

Thus international trade policy and competition policy have similar basic goals—to advance overall economic welfare or standards of living—but work to achieve those goals through diametrically different instruments. Trade policy seeks to avoid strategic behavior and secure *cooperative* solutions among trading nations; competition policy fosters *noncooperative* solutions among the business enterprises facing one another in the marketplace. There is many a slip between what the policymakers and implementers should do and what they actually do. But that is a theme addressed in subsequent chapters.

---

8. See, for example, Tirole (1988, chaps. 5–9); and Scherer and Ross (1990, chaps. 6–10).
9. As Hicks (1935, p. 8) quipped, "The best of all monopoly profits is a quiet life."

Chapter 2

National Trade Strategies and International Trade Policy

*T*HE STRATEGIES nations have pursued toward imports, exports, and foreign direct investment and (only recently) multilateral efforts to harmonize trading relationships have coexisted uneasily. A brief historical survey will illuminate some points of tension and rapprochement.

The Early Policy Debate

Two centuries ago, mercantilism was the dominant dogma concerning international trade and the strategies nations should adopt toward it.[1] The mercantilists perceived cross-border trade as a kind of zero-sum game: if nation A gained by accumulating a substantial trade surplus, its trading partner nation B lost commensurately. From this view the mercantilists concluded that nations should strive to achieve export surpluses and in that way to increase their stocks of gold and silver—the principal monetary metals. Implicit or explicit in this belief was the assumption that nations had unemployed or underemployed resources, especially labor. Through tariffs and quotas limiting imports and subsidies for exports, outlets would be found for additional production, and the monetary metals gained through trading would stimulate domestic economic activity and hence employment. Also, the gold and silver accumulated by running trade surpluses could be taxed or borrowed to enhance national power, among other things financing a remarkable and seemingly endless series of foreign adventures and wars.[2]

Adam Smith's *Wealth of Nations* was first and foremost a challenge to mercantilist principles. In his view, the main purpose of economic activ-

1. This section draws from Scherer and Belous (1994).
2. See Kennedy (1987, esp. chap. 3).

ity was to satisfy consumers' wants for goods and services, not to pile up monetary hoards. Smith showed that specialization in production could be combined with people's natural propensity to "truck and barter"—that is, to exchange goods and services—to make the citizens within a particular nation more prosperous. He went on to apply the same logic to foreign trade, viewing it as what we would now call a positive-sum game:

> What is prudence in the conduct of every private family, can scarce be folly in that of a great kingdom. If a foreign country can supply us with a commodity cheaper than we ourselves can make it, better buy it of them with some part of the produce of our own industry, employed in a way in which we have some advantage.[3]

Thus emerged the rudiments of the doctrine of comparative advantage, whose logic was further articulated in David Ricardo's *Principles of Political Economy* (1817) and many subsequent works by classical and neoclassical economists. Slowly but surely, the arguments of Smith and, more important, Ricardo (who was a member of the British Parliament) gained favor, at least in England. In 1828 Parliament weakened the Corn Laws protecting British agriculture, among other things reducing the cost of food for the workers in English manufacturing industry, which had ascended to a position of world leadership. In 1846, as the Irish famine gained momentum and other European grain supplies proved increasingly unreliable, Great Britain moved to an essentially free trade policy by repealing the last vestiges of the Corn Laws.

Meanwhile, a third emerging school of thought proved less eager to follow the free trade drummer. A seminal contribution came from Alexander Hamilton, the first secretary of the treasury in the newly independent United States. In his brilliant *Report on the Subject of Manufactures,* he argued:

> Not only the wealth; but the independence and security of a Country, appear to be materially connected with the prosperity of manufactures. Every nation, with a view to those great objects, ought to endeavor to possess within itself all the essentials of national supply. These comprise the means of *Subsistence habitation clothing* and *defence.*[4]

Because the British government had discouraged manufacturing in colonial America to increase its own exports, Hamilton believed that American manufacturers suffered a substantial handicap in any competition "with those who have previously attained to perfection in the business to

3. Smith ([1776] 1937, bk. 4, chap. 2, p. 424).
4. Hamilton ([1791] 1966, p. 291).

be attempted"—that is, relative to British industry.[5] To help manufacturers grow to a position of strength, he proposed protective tariffs, quotas, and subsidies, at the same time encouraging the importation of advanced foreign technology by letting manufacturing materials enter duty-free. In the short run, he admitted, manufactured goods would be provided to the citizens of America at high costs and prices. But in a prescient statement of what is now called the theory of learning by doing, he maintained that the long-run outcome would be quite different:

> There remains to be noticed an objection to the encouragement of manufactures, of a nature different from those which question the probability of success. This is derived from its supposed tendency to give a monopoly . . . to particula[r] classes at the expense of the rest of the community, who, it is affirmed, would be able to procure the requisite supplies of manufactured articles on better terms from foreigners, than from our own Citizens. . . .
>
> It is not an unreasonable supposition, that measures, which serve to abridge the free competition of foreign Articles, have a tendency to occasion an enhancement of prices and it is not to be denied that such is the effect in a number of Cases. . . . [But] the contrary is the ultimate effect with every successful manufacture. When a domestic manufacture has attained to perfection, and has engaged in the prosecution of it a competent number of Persons, it invariably becomes cheaper. . . . The internal competition, which takes place, soon does away every thing like Monopoly, and by degrees reduces the price of the Article to the *minimum* of a reasonable profit on the Capital employed.[6]

While exiled temporarily in America from his native Württemberg for criticizing governmental bureaucracy and advocating the privatization of state enterprises, Friedrich List read the work of Hamilton and began to embroider upon it, leading in 1841 to a magnum opus on national trade strategies.[7] "A new unprotected manufacturing power," List observed, "cannot possibly be raised up under free competition with a power which has long since grown in strength and is protected on its own territory."[8] List saw the Smithian free trade policies advocated by England as a ruse perpetrated to induce other nations' imitation, which would prevent them from matching England's industrial power.[9] List advocated protec-

---

5. Hamilton ([1791] 1966, p. 266).
6. Hamilton ([1791] 1966, pp. 285–86). Hamilton would allow tariffs to be so high as to prohibit imports only in cases when "a manufacture has made such a progress and is in so many hands as to insure a due competition" (p. 297).
7. List ([1841] 1916).
8. List ([1841] 1916, p. 117).
9. List ([1841] 1916, pp. 20, 295).

tion for "infant industries" in Germany, newly united under the Zoll-verein (customs union) of 1834, until they were able to hold their own in world industrial goods markets. Writing a half century after Hamilton, he also saw more clearly the relationship of science and technology to industrial power:

> There scarcely exists a manufacturing business which has not relations to physics, mechanics, chemistry, mathematics, or to the art of design, &c. No progress, no new discoveries and inventions, can be made in these sciences by which a hundred industries and processes could not be improved or altered. In the manufacturing State, therefore, sciences and arts must necessarily become popular. The necessity for education . . . induces men of special talents to devote themselves to instruction and authorship.[10]

Thus List urged the cultivation of science and the development of vocational education to help emerging German industries move to the technological frontiers—elements that still play an important role in explaining German industrial strength.

The writings of Hamilton and List established a foundation for what, with considerable further articulation, we now call "industrial policy." They also anticipated newer economic analyses exploring the strategies companies and nations adopt to gain international comparative advantage and shape the terms of trade, namely, "strategic trade policy." The tension recognized by List among such industrial policies, strategic trade policies, and Smith-Ricardo free trade policies has, if anything, grown. It is a recurring theme in what follows, especially in chapter 4.

National Trading Strategies and International Agreements

"The ideas of economists and political philosophers," John Maynard Keynes observed, "both when they are right and when they are wrong, are more powerful than is commonly understood. Indeed the world is ruled by little else."[11] During much of the nineteenth century, England followed the free trade maxims of Smith and Ricardo. Although there were intermittent policy fluctuations, America and Germany hewed more closely to Hamil-tonian and Listian policies than to the free trade alternative. After the U.S. Civil War, U.S. tariff policy was explicitly protectionist, although somewhat more so under Republican than under Democratic governments.[12] Ger-

10. List ([1841] 1916, p. 162).
11. Keynes (1936, p. 383).
12. For estimated average U.S. tariff rates between 1850 and 1890, see Hazlett (1992, p. 270).

many retreated from high-tariff policies in 1865 after indirectly embracing the Cobden commercial treaty of 1860 between England and France, but turned protectionist again following the worldwide depression of the 1870s.[13] Japan's economy was essentially closed until Commodore Matthew Perry's "black ships" arrived in 1853, and after that, Japan continued to protect its domestic industry through tariffs and informal trade barriers. Because it is impossible to survey developments in every nation, I emphasize those four in attempting to understand why diverse national policies emerged, and especially in probing the interface between national trading strategies and competition policies.

The early 1930s marked a decisive turning point in national trading policies. The Hawley-Smoot Tariff Act of 1930, which raised average U.S. tariffs to more than 50 percent, is widely considered to have aggravated the worldwide depression that commenced a year earlier. In 1934 Congress reversed field and passed the Reciprocal Trade Agreements Act, which permitted the president to negotiate substantial tariff reductions with nations that agreed to reciprocate with respect to U.S. exports.

Having recognized the harm done by Hawley-Smoot, and having attained, as England did in the early nineteenth century, unambiguous world leadership in the manufacture of tradable goods, the United States emerged from World War II committed to further liberalization of world trade. Rejecting the Listian view that advancing from a position of inferior manufacturing capability required protection, the leaders of several other industrialized nations were similarly inclined. Multilateral cooperation, it was recognized, could be more effective than bilateral negotiations in reducing barriers. Ratification of the GATT Treaty by 23 nations in 1947 and 1948 accelerated the tariff barrier dismantling process. Other nations followed suit, so that by 1993 GATT had 117 signatory nations. Further tariff-reducing steps were taken in several stages, including the Kennedy Round of negotiations during the 1960s; the Tokyo Round, concluded in 1979; and most recently the Uruguay Round, from which the agreements concluded in December 1993 remain to be ratified. Between 1947 and 1980, U.S. tariff rates were reduced by more than 85 percent.[14] It is estimated that average tariffs among GATT industrialized nations were reduced from approximately 40 percent in the late 1940s to 5 percent in the late 1980s.[15]

13. See, for example, Stolper, Häuser, and Borchardt (1967, pp. 34–34).

14. Ball (1993, chart 4).

15. See, for example, "Schools Brief: That Trade Winds May Blow Fair," *The Economist,* February 20, 1988, p. 81; and Keith Bradsher, "What's What in the World Trade Talks," *New York Times,* December 3, 1993, p. D17.

Although more than 100 nations joined GATT and the tariff reduction processes it facilitated, many accepted the call to free and open trade with reservations. Japan is perhaps the most important and interesting exception. During the late 1940s, there was a heated debate within the Japanese government over industrial development strategies.[16] Economists at the Japanese central bank urged that, by the logic of neoclassical comparative advantage theory, Japan should take advantage of its abundant low-wage labor and emphasize the production of labor-intensive products such as textiles and ceramics. Ministry of Trade and Industry (MITI) representatives argued in reply that if this strategy were chosen, Japan would remain an underdeveloped nation. Only by embracing new, advanced technologies in which Japan had no immediate comparative advantage, they insisted, could Japanese industry develop and join the ranks of the leading industrialized nations. The technology-forcing strategy was chosen. Medium- and high-technology industries were accorded substantial tariff and other protection against import competition until they had approached the technological frontier and could hold their own in world markets. Thus the Japanese industrial strategy hewed much more closely to the guidance of Hamilton and List than to that of Adam Smith, David Ricardo, and their heirs.

The Expansion of Trade and Foreign Investment

As a consequence of GATT and related international policy changes, trade flows increased enormously. For the twenty-four member nations of OECD (the Organization for Economic Cooperation and Development), imports rose to 12.1 percent of gross domestic product, averaged over the period 1960–67. The comparable subsequent figures were 13.6 percent for 1968–73, 17.6 percent for 1974–79, and 18.7 percent for 1980–90.[17] Some nations, especially within Europe, achieved very high degrees of openness—for example, with imports during 1980–90 averaging 70.0 percent of GDP for Belgium, 53.2 percent for the Netherlands, 36.4 percent for Switzerland, 26.6 percent for Germany, and 22.4 percent for France. For the United States, import penetration was more modest, at 10.6 percent of GDP during 1980–90, but this represented a considerable step upward from 4.4 percent in 1960–67. Japan's importing proclivities grew less, averaging 9.7 percent of GDP in 1960–67 and 10.9 percent in 1980–90. Its export rate in the latter period was 12.7 percent.

16. See Freeman (1987, pp. 34–34); and Fransman (1990, pp. 24–25).
17. OECD (1992b, p. 72).

Another change was even more dramatic. Multinational enterprises (MNEs) began to appear in the late nineteenth century; for example, as the U.S.-based Singer sewing machine company opened its first full-scale European factory in Glasgow during 1869 and the Dutch predecessor of Shell Oil tapped oil reserves in Sumatra (1885) and Texas (1901).[18] Following World War II, there was a marked increase in companies' overseas investments. The United States led the foreign direct investment parade, but other nations followed suit and during the 1980s invested more in the United States than American firms invested abroad. By 1989, a United Nations team estimated, the sales of all national corporations' off-shore subsidiaries totaled $4.4 trillion—a sum 1.75 times the magnitude of all national exports, excluding cross-border transactions from one unit of a given company to another.[19]

More precise statistics exist on MNE operations by U.S. firms outside the United States and by the subsidiaries of non-U.S. parents within the United States.

The sales of U.S. nonbank corporations' offshore affiliates rose from $0.65 trillion in 1977 to $1.48 trillion, or 31 percent of the parents' worldwide sales, in 1990.[20] Those foreign affiliates employed 6.7 million people in 1990. U.S. parents exported from the United States in 1990 to their majority-owned overseas affiliates merchandise valued at $89.6 billion. Their majority-owned offshore units, in turn, shipped to the U.S. parents $75.4 billion of merchandise—in this case appearing as imports in the U.S. international trade accounts. Such intracompany imports amounted to 15 percent of total U.S. merchandise imports in 1990.

The U.S. sales of foreign-owned nonbank companies doing business in the United States rose sharply from $194 billion in 1977 to $1.18 trillion in 1990.[21] The foreign-owned units employed 4.7 million Americans in 1990, or roughly 4 percent of the civilian work force. Those affiliates exported from the United States to their parents merchandise valued at $37.8 billion. The merchandise imports from their parents were $137.5 billion, or 28 percent of total 1990 U.S. merchandise imports. Adding the imports of foreign subsidiaries from their parents and U.S. parents from their foreign subsidiaries, one finds that 43 percent of 1990 U.S. merchandise imports occurred within more or less closely controlled intracompany channels.

Foreign direct investment occurs in part through green-field plant construction, but mergers are often the principal propelling force. Dur-

---

18. See, for example, Wilkins (1970, p. 42); and Yergin (1991, pp. 73, 87).
19. United Nations (1992, pp. 54–55).
20. Mataloni (1992).
21. Bezirganian (1993).

ing the years 1988–92, enterprises with home bases outside the United States acquired 257 U.S. companies valued at $100 million or more each. On average, the U.S. company assets acquired by foreign enterprises totaled approximately $30 billion a year.[22] During those same years, U.S.-based companies acquired foreign businesses at an average annual rate of almost $15 billion a year.[23] One hundred forty-seven of the acquired foreign companies were valued at $100 million or more. The competition policy implications of such merger activity are discussed further in chapter 4.

One further trend must be noted. Industrial technology, like industrial goods and services, has moved across national borders with increasing fluidity. A change experienced by the United States is particularly noteworthy. Over the years 1963 through 1976, foreign-based corporations obtained on average 26.5 percent of the U.S. invention patents assigned to corporations.[24] By 1990 foreign corporation assignments had nearly doubled to 51.2 percent. Thus overseas sources have come to originate more than half of America's newly patented corporate inventions.

Implications

In a sense, Adam Smith has triumphed, albeit after a lag that even economists concerned with the long run would consider substantial. During the second half of the twentieth century, there has been a distinct movement toward freer, more open, trading relationships among the world's nations, large and small. International trade has been substantial and rising in relation to aggregate national output. There has been a parallel increase in direct investment by overseas firms in national markets once reached only by exporting. Foreign enterprises therefore leaven competitive conditions within national markets in three ways: by exporting at arm's length from their home base to local consumers, by importing to their local affiliates, and through the sale of goods produced by their affiliates within a national market.

Despite these powerful trends, international trading relationships remain some distance short of the Smithian ideal. Tariff barriers have been replaced by other barriers to trade and foreign direct investment, some more subtle, others less so. Nations continue to pursue strategies that

22. Merrill Lynch Business Brokerage and Valuation (1993, p. 50). The $30 billion average is a lower-bound estimate, since it counts only acquisitions for which transaction prices were available.

23. Merrill Lynch (1993, p. 58).

24. National Science Board (1992, p. 430).

attempt to protect and nourish their national champion enterprises and turn the terms of trade in their favor through competition-distorting interventions. The lessons taught by Alexander Hamilton and Friedrich List have been applied with impressive ingenuity. GATT's Uruguay Round tried to dismantle some of the remaining barriers and distortions, but left many others untouched. And most important of all for the discussion here, the conflicts between national trading strategies, international trade policy, and competition policies were scarcely addressed.

Chapter 3

The Adoption of National and Transnational Competition Policies

I TURN NOW from international trade strategies and policies to a much newer phenomenon, competition policies. This chapter examines the historical events that precipitated the adoption of national and transnational competition policies, paying particular attention to the climate of ideas within which those policies emerged. Like chapter 2, this chapter focuses on four nations, the United States, the United Kingdom, Germany, and Japan, not only because of their prominence in the world economy but because their early policy choices differed so dramatically. The discussion then moves on to review the efforts, some successful and some not, to enact competition policies spanning national borders.

The Early U.S. Experience

The United States was the first "common market" of continental scale. In one sense, the United States became a common market in 1789 when the Constitution was ratified, replacing the Articles of Confederation, under which the individual states could impose tariffs and other legal barriers against imports from peer states. But trade among the post-Constitution states was impeded by physical barriers. Roads were primitive, and inland waterways were often impassible during winter freezes and summer droughts. The physical integration of the American continental market advanced by leaps and bounds during the second half of the nineteenth century. One significant contributor was the extension of the railroads, from 9,000 miles of road operated in 1850 to 167,000 miles in 1890.[1] Communication improved apace as telegraph lines were

1. U.S. Department of Commerce, Bureau of the Census (1960, p. 427).

17

strung (growing from 76,000 miles in 1866 to 679,000 in 1890),[2] after which telephone service proliferated. As transportation and communication costs fell, it became possible for the first time to ship merchandise swiftly and economically to the whole U.S. market from a single location. Manufacturers responded with technological and organizational innovations permitting previously unattainable scale economy and firm size frontiers to be probed. As Alfred Chandler observes:

> The laying down of railway and telegraph systems precipitated a wave of industrial innovation in western Europe and the United States far more wide-ranging than that which had occurred in Britain at the end of the eighteenth century. This wave has been properly termed by historians the Second Industrial Revolution.[3]

The explosive growth, by both internal expansion and merger, of numerous leading American enterprises to unprecedented size transformed U.S. market structures, the behavioral strategies adopted by firms, and public perceptions about the proper relationship between government and business. These developments led to the passage of twelve state antitrust laws and then to the first U.S. federal antitrust law, the Sherman Antitrust Act of 1890.

When the Sherman Act was passed, about 40 percent of the U.S. work force was engaged in farming. The "trusts" were seen by farmers to have elevated industrial product prices relative to farm product prices (which fell during the 1880s, largely for macroeconomic reasons). The first states to enact antitrust laws in 1889 and 1890 were preponderantly agricultural.[4] That antitrust legislation was a child of the prairie frontier is suggested by the fact that the only analogous early antitrust laws were passed in Canada (in 1899) and Australia (in 1906). For a variety of reasons, however, the Canadian and Australian laws were enforced only sporadically, so the more significant U.S. experience is emphasized here.[5]

Discontent over the actions of the "trusts" spread beyond the prairies, however. Through predatory pricing, the trusts were said to have driven many small firms out of business, and it was with small business that the public's sentiments lay. The fortunes built upon monopoly profits in-

2. U.S. Department of Commerce, Bureau of the Census (1960, p. 484).
3. Chandler (1990, p. 62).
4. They were Kansas, Iowa, Kentucky, Maine, Michigan, Mississippi, Missouri, Nebraska, North Dakota, South Dakota, Tennessee, and Texas. See Millon (1990).
5. See Dunlop, McQueen, and Trebilcock (1987, pp. 18–22); and Blakeney and Patfield (1991, sec. 1.01). The proximate impetus to Australian legislation is said to have been alleged dumping of farm implements in Australia by the U.S.-based International Harvester Company.

creased the inequality of income distribution, evoking reactions particularly bitter because of the way wealth was flaunted then by those who possessed it. During the late 1880s, liberal newspapers editorialized regularly against the trusts, and in the 1888 presidential election all of the major parties included antitrust planks in their platforms.[6]

The formation of market-dominating trusts was nearly unique to the United States, mirrored on a much smaller scale in England. In the rest of Europe, the preponderant reaction to the changes in transportation, communication, and industrial technology was the formation of more loosely structured cartels. As the cartelization and trust movements gained momentum during the closing decades of the nineteenth century, economists probed deeply and debated vigorously the events unfolding before them. At the time the Sherman Act was passed, there were differences of opinion on four important economic issues: economies of scale, the abusiveness of pricing, preferred reform strategies, and the question whether the alternative to cartels and monopolies would be even worse.

Some leading economists, such as America's John Bates Clark and England's Alfred Marshall, saw the new industrial forms as dinosaur-like mutations whose long-term viability would be determined by natural selection.[7] Reliable information on the cost advantages of the trusts, and hence on their long-term survivability, began to accumulate only during the last decade of the century, after the Sherman Act was passed.[8] Marshall in England and Richard T. Ely of Johns Hopkins University were skeptical of the trusts' superior efficiency. So was Charles Bullock of Harvard, reviewing the evidence on scale economies and managerial diseconomies at the turn of the century.[9] Arthur Hadley of Yale, on the other hand, perceived the large new organizations' cost and other advantages to be so compelling that to "control the abuses without destroying the industries is a matter of the utmost difficulty."[10] A view similar to Hadley's, but even stronger, was held by Robert Liefmann, the leading industrial organization economist of the German-speaking world. Given this divergence of opinions, even noneconomist Theodore Roosevelt expressed views surprisingly inconsistent with his role as the American president who gave antitrust its structural sting:

6. For an analysis of the early history, see Thorelli (1954); and Letwin (1965).

7. The interpretations here are drawn from a compilation of articles by the intellectual leaders of the late nineteenth century in Scherer (1993). See also Scherer (1990).

8. The beginning of a new era of understanding was the Chicago Trust Conference of 1899. See Hatfield (1899).

9. Bullock (1901); reprinted in Scherer (1993, vol. 2, pp. 5–55).

10. Hadley (1887); reprinted in Scherer (1993, vol. 1, p. 30). Hadley later became president of Yale University.

This is an era of combination. Big business has come to stay. It cannot be put an end to; and if it could be put an end to, it would mean the most widespread disaster to the community. . . . No great industrial well-being can come unless big business prospers. . . . We cannot hold our own with foreign competition, we cannot lead in developing South America, without successful big business concerns.[11]

Whatever their interpretation of the market shares needed to exhaust scale economies, nearly all serious scholars believed that the newly created monopolies abused their power. They differed on how serious that abuse was. Some claimed that fear of potential competition led the more far-sighted trusts to hold their prices to reasonable levels. Others disagreed and emphasized both the price-raising effects and the severe and unfair price discrimination in which many trusts engaged.

There were differences too on remedies. Some (such as Richard Ely) favored nationalization in cases where the cost advantages of size led to natural monopoly; others advocated public regulation;[12] many believed that the worst abuses would be avoided if the government forced the corporations to make public detailed information on their prices, profits, and financial structure. The possibilities of what became antitrust were poorly comprehended. Nevertheless, I have been able to find no leading economist of the time who urged strict laissez faire toward monopolistic consolidations.[13]

Perhaps the most crucial difference among economists turned on whether under emerging industrial conditions free competition tended to be "cutthroat" and "ruinous," or whether there were effective restorative mechanisms. In the United States, Arthur Hadley was a forceful spokesman for the ruinous competition school, which appears to have been a minority position among economists, if not among businessmen. He argued that, given the high fixed costs typical of the new industrial enterprises, entrepreneurs would compete their prices down to their low variable costs, incurring substantial and destructive losses until cartels or trusts were formed to rescue the situation. In Germany, Liefmann carried the argument further, emphasizing that when the cartels raised prices, new entry flooded in, undermining the price front and triggering

11. *Roosevelt, Works of Theodore* (1925, pp. 72–73). To be sure, this view was expressed eight years after Roosevelt left the presidency, and after he pointedly criticized other presidents' antitrust policies.

12. Theodore Roosevelt adhered to this school in his postpresidential years; for example, "The proper thing to do is to socialize [big business], to make it more an agent for social good, and to do away with everything in it that tends toward social evil. To do this there must be a wise governmental control." *Roosevelt, Works* (1925, p. 72).

13. Compare Stigler (1982).

another round of price warfare. Cartels or monopoly consolidations were necessary under modern industrial conditions, Liefmann believed, but their destructive propensities had to be regulated by the government. Liefmann's was by far the most prominent voice on cartel economics in Germany, whereas in the United States those who listened to the economists heard a confusing Babel. It seems plausible that the relative homogeneity of intellectual views favored pro-cartel policies in Germany, whereas in the United States the lack of consensus permitted the Sherman Act's cartel prohibitions to be enacted by legislators, and interpreted by judges, among whom only the cries of abuse remained undisputed.

The early trusts also resonated badly against a political philosophy with uniquely deep roots in America. The legislators who passed the Sherman Act, and perhaps especially those from agrarian states, inherited the U.S. founding fathers' dislike of oppressive governmental power. In Federalist Paper 10, James Madison argued that it was important to curb the exercise of power elicited from government by strong factions, and especially by economic interest groups.[14] Factions could be kept diffuse, and hence with limited political power, Madison believed, by forming a large republic out of many small ones—in economic terms, by broadening the market. Under eighteenth-century industrial conditions, the political clout of a specific "manufacturing interest" or "mercantile interest" would then be checked almost automatically. This aversion to power persisted under the quite different industrial conditions of 1890. Thus, as Senator Sherman said in his principal address supporting his original bill:

> If anything is wrong this [industrial combination] is wrong. If we will not endure a king as a political power we should not endure a king over the production, transportation, and sale of any of the necessaries of life. If we would not submit to an emperor we should not submit to an autocrat of trade, with power to prevent competition and to fix the price of any commodity.[15]

Or as Senator Hoar complained, "these great monopolies . . . are a menace to republican institutions."[16]

Shortly before passing the Sherman Act, Congress raised U.S. import tariffs to an unprecedented average level of 51 percent.[17] One interpretation of this coincidence is that Congress, recognizing that higher import barriers facilitated price-raising by domestic monopolies, saw the need

14. The paper is reprinted in Scherer (1993, pp. 20–29).
15. *Congressional Record,* vol. 21 (1890), p. 2457.
16. *Congressional Record,* vol. 21 (1890), p. 3146.
17. See Hazlett (1992, p. 270).

for a countervailing measure.[18] Thomas Hazlett's more cynical view is that the Sherman Act was merely a cosmetic palliative giving legislators a talking point to pacify constituents injured as a result of higher tariffs.[19]

Palliative or not, the Sherman Act contained strong language directed toward restrictive agreements and monopolistic combinations. Section 1 declared to be illegal "every contract, combination . . . or conspiracy, in restraint of trade or commerce among the several States, or with foreign nations." Section 2 prescribed fines, or imprisonment, or both, for every person (including legal persons) who "shall monopolize or attempt to monopolize . . . any part of the trade or commerce among the several States, or with foreign nations."

Enforcement by the Harrison and Cleveland administrations was at first unenthusiastic and perhaps incompetent.[20] The law itself was phrased in general terms, and because the debates in Congress were at best confusing, it was possible to draw wildly different inferences about what Congress actually intended.[21] Much hinged on interpretations supplied by the courts. An early federal district court opinion, echoing the widely disseminated views of Senator George Hoar,[22] concluded:

> When [price-fixing] contracts go to the extent only of preventing unhealthy competition, and yet at the same time furnish the public with adequate facilities at fixed and reasonable prices, and are made only for the purpose of averting personal ruin, the contract is lawful.[23]

But when the same leading case was appealed by a more zealous new attorney general, the Supreme Court articulated a much different standard:

> When . . . the body of an act pronounces as illegal every contract or combination in restraint of trade or commerce . . . the plain and ordinary meaning . . . is not limited to that kind of contract alone which is in unreasonable restraint of trade, but all contracts are included in such language, and no exception or limitation can be added without placing in the act that which has been omitted by congress. . . . It may be that the policy evidenced by the passage of the

18. When Henry Havemeyer, president of the American Sugar Refining Company, said in 1899 that "the mother of all trusts is the customs tariff bill"—a declaration widely repeated as "the tariff is the mother of trusts"—he probably implied the following nexus: tariffs led to an elevation of domestic prices, which induced an overreacting flood of entry, which triggered a price war, which in turn led to cartelization or consolidation. See Zerbe (1969, p. 341); and Taussig (1900).

19. Hazlett (1992, p. 273).

20. See Letwin (1965, chap. 4).

21. Compare Bork (1966) with Lande (1982, pp. 65–151).

22. See Tarbell (1925, p. 99).

23. *U.S. v. Trans-Missouri Freight Association et al.*, 53 Fed. 440, 451 (1892).

[Sherman] act itself will, if carried out, result in disaster to the [rail]roads. . . . These considerations are, however, not for us.[24]

And even though the Supreme Court divided by five to four in its opinion, this unqualified prohibition, known in legal terms as a "per se rule," endured and became the law of the land.

Further invigoration came after Theodore Roosevelt became president in 1901. Under Roosevelt, special investigative and enforcement organs were established, a merger between the Great Northern and Northern Pacific railroads was enjoined, and a suit was brought against the grandfather of American trusts, the Standard Oil Company. When the Supreme Court ruled in 1911 that Standard Oil had violated the Sherman Act and must be broken into thirty-four separate companies, it became clear that, whatever its intent had been, Congress had created a powerful antimonopoly weapon. The weapon was wielded with widely fluctuating aggressiveness by subsequent administrations, and in the depths of the Depression total disarmament occurred.[25] But a further policy turn followed in 1938, revealing that once a weapon's blueprint exists, power can be restored quickly.

Parallel Developments in Other Nations

The 1890s and 1900s brought fundamental competition policy choices in other nations too. Those choices diverged dramatically from the policies adopted in the United States. It is important to understand why.

Germany

Germany represents an opposite extreme in the choice of policies. As German competition law emerged during the 1890s, cartel agreements were recognized as legally permissible and indeed enforceable in court under some circumstances against members that sought to defect from agreements they had entered previously. This legal view interacted with economic changes of the time to induce an enormous proliferation of cartels. In 1875, it is estimated, there were 8 formal German cartels; in 1887, 70. By 1905, an official survey counted 395 cartels.[26]

---

24. *U.S. v. Trans-Missouri Freight Association*, 166 U.S. 290, 328, 340 (1897). Section 1 of the Sherman Act prohibited "*every* contract, combination . . . or conspiracy, in restraint of trade."

25. Hawley (1966).

26. Voigt (1962, pp. 170–74).

The first definitive statement on the legality of the new cartel forms was issued by the German high court (Reichsgericht) in 1897. Considering a case involving the wood pulp manufacturers of Saxony, the court ruled that cartel agreements were lawful and binding under the freedom of association accorded workers and businesses under German law. Only in special cases where a cartel led to an "actual monopoly," or where there was extreme exploitation of consumers—a situation not observed in the case at hand—might the courts take anticartel action.[27] Eleven years later the court returned to the cartel question and, ordering that the members of a construction cartel adhere to their agreement, provided a clear statement of how far the German law differed from its American counterpart:

> Since it has become customary for public organizations to allocate work on the basis of minimum bids responding to advertised specifications, unrestrained competition from dishonest underbidding poses a serious danger for the condition of tradesmen. Agreements among businessmen whose purpose is to mitigate this danger and maintain appropriate prices offend public morals so little that from the standpoint of a healthy economy, they deserve general approval. . . . Setting minimum offer prices with the understanding that the other cartel members must bid higher is an obvious element of such agreements. Keeping them secret is also natural. . . . And when a public official is actually misled by such secret understandings, he has only his own negligent comprehension of how business is done to blame.[28]

It is unclear whether these judicial decisions were mirroring the opinion of informed scholars, or whether scholarly writings fell into line with the general spirit of the times. As noted earlier, the leading contemporary German student of cartel economics was Robert Liefmann. Liefmann's doctoral dissertation on cartels appeared in 1897, the year in which the German high court rendered its first cartel decision. Liefmann saw unrestricted competition as inherently unstable and the advantages of cartelization to be compelling. In a 1902 paper written to inform parliamentary debates on the cartel problem, Liefmann stated as basic principles:

> The right to unite is for the worker as for the entrepreneur the fundamental condition for every element of progress in the economy. . . . Cartels are a necessary phenomenon in our current economy, and it can never be the function of the State to suppress them, but only to hinder as much as possible their unfavorable effects.[29]

27. See Niederleithinger (1985).
28. Niederleithinger (1985, p. 8). The translation is mine.
29. Quoted in Blaich (1974, pp. 142–43). The translation is mine.

Liefmann's views were apparently widely shared by other German economists. At a discussion of cartels by the Verein für Sozialpolitik (German Economic Association) in 1905, the most eminent German economist of the time, Gustav Schmoller, feared that the decline of competition through cartelization would lead to a socialistic state.[30] However, while condemning American trusts, Schmoller praised the economic advantages and "discipline" of German cartels—a judgment in which Liefmann concurred.[31]

Even before the German high court issued its first cartel decision, the German Reichstag (parliament) wrestled in open session with a monopoly problem not unfamiliar to Americans: the Standard Oil Company. After waging a price war that led to its acquisition of all independent German petroleum product importers, Standard Oil raised the price of imported kerosene from 12.62 to 19.00 marks per hundred kilograms in April 1895.[32] Because vast numbers of Germans depended upon kerosene for illumination, the price increase evoked outrage, and parliamentary debates over Standard Oil's monopoly position took place in 1895 and 1897. But the delegates found themselves hopelessly at odds over what to do.

One specialist in economic matters argued that the Standard organization realized vast scale economies, permitting petroleum products to be sold at lower prices than under a less concentrated industry organization. Because the 1895 price increase was quickly rescinded, perhaps partly in fear of evoking substitute competition from gas illumination and alcohol lamps, several participants believed that Standard would continue to charge modest prices. Liberals disagreed. Representatives of agrarian interests believed high cartelized kerosene prices would be a good thing, since then substitution would occur from alcohol produced using the wheat their constituents grew. Social Democrats pointed out that if laws were enacted to attack a monopolistic organization such as Standard Oil, consistency would require similar measures toward the Rheinland-Westphalen coal syndicate, whose cartel organization allowed it to pay its workers higher wages, and the potash syndicate, which was a major source of export earnings (in considerable measure, on shipments to the United States).[33] The ruling Conservatives endorsed this view from a different perspective, emphasizing the desire to maintain freedom of contract. A suggestion that Germany foster the development of its own petroleum refining industry by raising tariffs on refined products and

30. Voigt (1962, p. 174).
31. Blaich (1974, p. 146).
32. Blaich (1970).
33. Potash continued to pose problems for German competition policy enforcers in 1993. See "Germany's Antitrust Enforcement Chief Reflects on Mergers and Privatization," *Antitrust and Trade Regulation Report*, August 19, 1993, pp. 278–79.

reducing them on crude oil elicited fear of American tariff retaliation and concern that kerosene prices would nevertheless rise.

Unable to agree, and informed that Standard Oil had consented to eliminate the exclusive dealing requirements it had imposed upon its distributors, the parliament decided to refrain from enacting any cartel legislation, in effect allowing the permissive policy articulated by the Reichsgericht to persist. But the Prussian and Hessian railroads reduced their freight rates on oil from Russia by nearly two-thirds, as a result of which Russian imports rose from under 5 percent of total German consumption in 1893 to over 10 percent in 1899.

Not until 1923 did the Reichstag enact a cartel law—a step that was more a panic-stricken reaction to hyperinflation than the consequence of any new understanding of how cartels functioned. The new law closely followed the recommendations Robert Liefmann had been advancing for more than two decades. Cartels were required to register with a newly created administrative agency, which could seek the correction of abuses case-by-case before a new Cartel Court—a power exercised sparingly in subsequent years.[34] The court also had jurisdiction over petitions by individual cartel members to withdraw from their agreements when those agreements unfairly restricted their freedom of action. In 1930, to combat what for Germany was a particularly severe depression, participation in cartels was made compulsory for vulnerable industries. Later in that decade compulsory cartelization was made even more comprehensive by the Hitler government, among other things to organize German war-making capabilities.

England

From the year 1599 on, English courts looked with disfavor on monopolies conferred by a grant of royal privilege.[35] The Statute of Monopolies in 1624 specified inventions as the principal exception. Early English common law also frowned upon attempts to corner a market but approved voluntary agreements not to compete (for example, when an apprentice left his master's shop, or a master sold his business to another) if reasonably limited in time and space. In the ninetenth century, laws were passed making it legal for both workers and masters to combine in negotiating wages and working conditions. Agreements among sellers to avoid price competition and restrain entry remained on more uncertain ground until 1889. In that year the Court of Appeals ruled that concerted actions undertaken for the sake of business advantage could not secure

34. See Voigt (1962, p. 178).
35. For an excellent survey, see Letwin (1965, chap. 2).

the enforcement aid of the courts, but unless they injured rival businesses through fraud, intimidation, or molestation, the courts would not reach out to enjoin them.[36] Thus cartel agreements were permitted, but they would not be given the active support offered under German law.

Japan

In Japan, as in Germany, both economists and public officials tended to see unfettered competition as unstable and ruinous.[37] Ryutaro Komiya, a perceptive observer of Japanese economic policy, relates the desire to ameliorate "excessive" competition more fundamentally to Confucian notions of order and harmony.[38] Government officials were anxious to avoid disturbances, bankruptcies, and claims for administrative succor. Intervention by hierarchical government authorities to bring order to business activities was viewed positively, not negatively as under the Madisonian tradition of the United States. Japanese government agencies therefore favored cartelization under the banner of avoiding excessive competition and acted in many instances to induce cooperation among Japanese enterprises and consolidation into the family groupings known as *Zaibatsu* (literally, money cliques). The ensuing relationships among contending Zaibatsu groups, according to William Lockwood, exhibited

> a rather indeterminate blend of sharp jealousy and mutual solidarity, of rugged individualism and collusive action. If rivalries were keen, they yet operated in a setting characterized by a propensity among the rivals to cooperate in abating the rigors of the free market.[39]

Nothing that approximates modern competition policy laws is known to have existed in Japan during the late nineteenth century and the period before World War II.

Other Nations

At a conference of the Inter-Parliamentary Union held in London in 1930, it was ascertained that only two European nations—Germany and Norway—had specific statutes seeking to control cartels and monopo-

36. The key case was *Mogul Steamship Co.* v. *McGregor, Gow & Co. et al.*, 23 Q.B.D. 598 (1889), affirmed A.C. 25 (1892); analyzed by Letwin (1965, pp. 49–51).

37. For a clear statement of Japanese views and one of the first known expressions of skepticism, see Niino (1962); reprinted in Scherer (1993, vol. 1, pp. 178–89).

38. Komiya (1990, pp. 297–301); reprinted in Scherer (1993, vol. 1, pp. 190–95). See also the perceptive analysis by Wolfrum (1991, pp. 5–10).

39. Lockwood (1968, p. 231).

lies.[40] The European participants unanimously adopted a resolution that stated:

> Cartels, trusts and other analogous combines are natural phenomena of economic life towards which it is impossible to adopt an entirely negative attitude. Seeing, however, that those combines may have a harmful effect both as regards public interests and those of the State, it is necessary that they should be controlled. This Control should not take the form of an interference in economic life likely to affect its normal development. It should simply seek to establish a supervision over possible abuses and to prevent those abuses.[41]

Cartel legislation was in fact adopted by some European nations during the 1930s—for example, by Denmark (1931), the Netherlands 1935), and Austria (1938, after the German Anschluss).[42] It and later European cartel laws tended to follow the German pattern, requiring registration, attempting to correct abuses (at most, occasionally), and in many instances encouraging the formation of cartels when market conditions proved to be unstable.

Changes in National Policy after World War II

Following World War II, there was at first a trickle and then a flood of legislation establishing national competition policies. Again, I emphasize a few particularly prominent examples.

Germany and Japan

When World War II ended, the victors, and especially the United States, sought to transplant U.S. antitrust notions in German and Japanese soil. Although changes occurred, as an exercise in free market proselytizing, the effort was bungled. At the Quebec conference of September 1944, Franklin D. Roosevelt and Winston Churchill agreed that to destroy German's war potential, "the industries in the Ruhr and the Saar would . . . necessarily be put out of action, closed down. . . . This program looks forward to converting Germany into a country principally agricul-

---

40. Boserup and Schlichtkrull (1962, p. 60). France had laws regulating price-fixing and related practices as early as 1791. As amended in 1926, the Napoleonic Penal Code condemned collective action to raise or lower prices artificially for the purpose of acquiring profit. See Edwards (1964, pp. 33–34). Its enforcement may have been so rare that the 1930 conference participants were unaware of its existence.

41. Reproduced in Boserup and Schlichtkrull (1962, p. 59).

42. Boserup and Schlichtkrull (1962, pp. 66–78).

tural and pastoral."[43] The Potsdam agreement of July 1945 stated, "At the earliest practicable date, the German economy shall be decentralized for the purpose of eliminating the present excessive concentration of economic power as exemplified in particular by cartels, syndicates, trusts and other monopolistic arrangements."[44] The 1947 occupation authority law implementing the Potsdam agreement prohibited restrictive and monopolistic enterprises and practices. Its preamble stated that the ordinance was issued to prevent Germany from "endangering the safety of her neighbors" and "to destroy Germany's economic potential to wage war."[45] If one suppresses cartels and monopolistic enterprises to eliminate economic power, what does one do to build economic power?

The question was hardly academic, as the United States and Great Britain realized when they decided to reverse field and rebuild German industry as a buttress against a new threat, the Soviet Union. After chemical giant I.G. Farben and the twelve largest coal and steel syndicates were dismembered, the western Allies backed off from their deconcentration program. Similarly, once ties among Zaibatsu enterprises were loosened, the United States abandoned its deconcentration efforts in Japan.[46] What was initially billed as a bully demonstration of competition policy had the paradoxical effect of inoculating German and Japanese public opinion against competition policy.

Despite this turn of events, West Germany passed in July 1957, following seven years of deliberation, one of the world's most stringent competition policy laws.[47] During the half century preceding World War II, as shown before, Germany had an extraordinarily strong *pro*-cartel law. The Bundestag (parliament) debate formed along two main battle lines.[48] One group believed that West Germany should return to the "abuse" philosophy embodied in the 1923 law—in effect, preserving the intellectual heritage of Robert Liefmann. Cartels would be permitted generally, but subject to oversight for abuses. The other "prohibitionist" group represented the newer Freiburg School, of whom Ludwig Erhard, the first economics minister (and later chancellor) of the postwar Federal Republic of Germany, was a strong adherent. Led by Walter Eucken and

43. Stolper, Häuser, and Borchardt (1967, pp. 181–82).

44. Stolper, Häuser, and Borchardt (1967, p. 194).

45. Law No. 56, "Prohibition of Excessive Concentration of German Economic Power," by order of the Military Government, December 2, 1947.

46. See Bisson (1954).

47. The German law's enactment followed ratification of the European Economic Community's Treaty of Rome by four months.

48. See Voigt (1962, pp. 190–91).

Franz Boehm,[49] and influenced by research on the distortions cartelization introduced into the German economy,[50] the Freiburg economists believed passionately in competitive free market processes. They believed too that strong tendencies toward monopoly could frustrate the attainment of competitive market order (*Marktordnung*), and that the government must therefore intervene to interdict cartels and monopolies. Central to their philosophy was a Madisonian distaste for the infringement of individual liberties by powerful interests—amplified in prior German history by the oppression that stemmed from powerful government, powerful cartels, and the two acting together.[51] Erhard preached the Freiburg gospel to skeptical German parliament members, securing passage of a tough compromise law and the formation of a Federal Cartel Office.[52] Like many new agencies, the Cartel Office tread warily at first, but in time took strong action against price-fixing agreements and other cartels not covered by exceptions.[53] The new law lacked structural fragmentation mandates analogous to those imposed by the Allies in 1947, but merger control provisions were added in a 1973 amendment.

In Japan, competition policy was imposed somewhat less clumsily by the occupying U.S. authorities following World War II. The 1947 "Act Concerning Prohibition of Private Monopoly and the Maintenance of Fair Trade," known more popularly as the Antimonopoly Law, was at least less pejoratively titled than its West German counterpart. The Zaibatsu dissolution program was also conducted under separate authority. When the U.S. occupation ended, the Antimonopoly Law was weakened substantially, but its title was maintained, as was its implementing agency, the Fair Trade Commission. Nevertheless, the law carried the stigma, as two Japanese authors observed a quarter century later, of a "foreign [implant]" imposed, "to suppress the economy of Japan so that it could

49. The contest was joined preliminarily in 1927, when Boehm, an official of the Cartel Office, wrote from his experience that legislators formulating cartel law needed to bring economic power under the law. In a critique, Liefmann argued that the concept of "economic power" was vague—the sort of thing that might come from sociologists rather than economists. Blaich (1974, p. 154). On Walter Eucken, see "Die Ordnung oder Freiheit" (1993).

50. See, for example, Bloch (1932), who observes that cartel-induced raw material price increases made downstream industries noncompetitive internationally and stimulated investment in excessive capacity.

51. On the role of big business in bringing the Hitler government to power, see Mann and Plummer (1991, pp. 81–83).

52. For more on the history, see Stolper and others (1967, pp. 46–49, 104–105, 258–59); Mestmäcker (1980); and Kaufer (1980).

53. Exceptions were allowed for structural crisis, rationalization, export, import, and conditions (that is, discount and payment terms) cartels. See chapter 4 in this volume.

not recover and grow."[54] Or, as an official Fair Trade Commission statement noted, the act was "considered to be one of the irresistible results of defeat and an act forced upon Japan."[55]

Amendments in 1953 relaxed some flat prohibitions so that they affected only actions *substantially* restraining competition, exempted depression and rationalization cartels, and weakened the provisions concerning resale price maintenance for differentiated products. Parallel new laws authorized cartels aimed at preventing excessive competition among small and medium-size enterprises (for example, those with fewer than 300 employees) and permitted the Ministry of Trade and Industry (MITI) to approve export and import cartels upon consultation with the Fair Trade Commission.[56]

During the first decades of its existence the Fair Trade Commission pursued its mandate timidly, relying upon persuasion rather than compulsion, and coordinated its efforts closely with other agencies such as MITI. In the late 1960s, however, pollution scandals and concern over what (at least in Japan) were considered rapid price increases led to the emergence of a consumer movement, which induced the government to increase the FTC's budget and to approve somewhat more vigorous challenges to price-fixing arrangements.[57] In 1969 the commission challenged a MITI-brokered merger between Yawata Steel and Fuji Iron and Steel, which had been separated under the postwar Zaibatsu dissolution program. The action drew threats from MITI to strip the commission of its merger enforcement authority, but eventually a compromise was reached under which the merger was consummated (creating Nippon Steel) with minor spinoffs and supply guarantees.[58] In 1974 the commission initiated its first criminal price-fixing case, against twelve petroleum refining companies. The companies defended themselves by insisting that they were acting under "administrative guidance" from MITI. After lengthy proceedings, the Japanese Supreme Court ruled in 1984 that agreements contrary to the Antimonopoly Act were exempt when they conformed to bona fide administrative guidance, but that the challenged petroleum product price-fixing activities did not follow such guidance and were therefore illegal.[59] Meanwhile, the commission was

54. Iyori and Uesugi (1983, p. vii); quoted in Wolfrum (1991, p. 15).

55. Fair Trade Commission (1973, p. 2).

56. In 1993 the Japanese Fair Trade Commission proposed that most of the exemptions be eliminated by 1995. "JFTC Expects to Propose Elimination of Cartels Now Exempt from Antitrust Attack," *Antitrust and Trade Regulation Report,* November 4, 1993, pp. 604–05.

57. See Imamura (1973, p. 291). For a more critical current evaluation, see "Japan's Fair Trade Commission: Pussycat," *The Economist,* October 23, 1993, pp. 85–86.

58. See "Japanese Fair Trade Commission Decision on the Yawata-Fuji Steel Merger" (1970).

59. OECD (1987, pp. 131–32).

authorized in 1977 to impose substantially increased fines, which were in fact levied in several subsequent cases.

The United Kingdom and Other Nations

In other nations, the postwar movement toward competition policies occurred without the compulsory element of military occupation.

In the United Kingdom, for example, a revision of policies prevailing since the 1890s was presaged by the publication of a white paper in 1944 warning that the attainment of postwar full employment objectives might be jeopardized by the price-fixing practices of cartels and monopolies.[60] In 1948 a Monopolies and Restrictive Practices Commission was created to analyze prominent monopoly conditions, publish reports on its findings, and make nonbinding recommendations for change. In 1956 a new Restrictive Trade Practices Act was passed. It prohibited restraints of trade among suppliers of goods,[61] specified exceptions or "gateways" to the prohibition, required registration of trade-restricting agreements with what is now called the Office of Fair Trading, and created a Restrictive Practices Court to adjudicate contested cases. A tough line was taken in early RPC decisions, and scores of formal restrictive agreements were abandoned.[62] Control of mergers entailing substantial market share accretions was assigned to the (renamed) Monopolies and Mergers Commission beginning in 1965.

The postwar competition policy developments in the United Kingdom, Germany, and Japan were emulated with rich variations in most other industrialized nations and in a handful of less-developed nations. Nations such as Canada that already had competition policy laws strengthened them and began enforcing them vigorously.[63] Other nations enacted new laws and then gradually broadened their scope and increased the intensity of enforcement. The OECD's competition policy reports for 1989–90 and 1990–1991 disclosed the existence or creation of active programs for twenty OECD member nations and the European Community.[64] Italy joined the fold in 1991, which left as holdouts only Turkey, Luxembourg, and Iceland—the last two being too small to justify the administrative cost. With the collapse of the Iron Curtain, competition policies also became a popular export to

60. George (1990, p. 105).

61. Services were added in 1974 amendments.

62. The 1956 law induced considerable adaptation toward more informal arrangements thought to escape censure. See Swann and others (1974, esp. chap. 4). On pending proposals for reform, see Hay and Vickers (1988).

63. For a survey as of 1963, with texts of the currently applicable German, French, Dutch, and Belgian laws, see U.S. Senate Judiciary Committee (1963, pt. 1, pp. 126–255).

64. OECD (1992a); OECD (1993a).

former Soviet bloc members. By the end of 1992, Hungary, Poland, Czechoslovakia, Bulgaria, Russia, and Lithuania had enacted competition policy statutes.[65]

Transnational Competition Policy: The European Community

As individual nations were enacting or strengthening their competition policies, there were parallel transnational initiatives. The most important developments occurred in the European Community (EC) and its precursor, the European Coal and Steel Community (ECSC).

When France, West Germany, Belgium, Holland, Italy, and Luxembourg joined to create the ECSC in 1951, the formative treaty prohibited (in its article 4)

(a) import and export duties . . . and quantitative restrictions on the movement of coal and steel;

(b) measures or practices discriminating among producers, among buyers, or among consumers . . . as well as . . . practices which hamper the buyer in the free choice of his supplier;

(c) subsidies or state assistance, or special charges imposed by the state . . . ;

(d) restrictive practices tending toward the division of markets or the exploitation of the consumer.[66]

Article 65 of the treaty prohibited agreements and concerted practices that tended to "prevent, restrict, or distort the normal operation of competition" within the Community. Article 66 contained provisions restricting "unauthorized concentrations" (such as large-scale mergers) and permitting the Community's High Authority to combat abuses by enterprises possessing a dominant market position. Thus, for the first time, a transnational competition policy was adopted in conjunction with trade liberalization within a trading bloc.

Robert Schumann's effort to organize the ECSC was apparently precipitated by the wartime victors' decision to rebuild German economic strength as a bulwark against Soviet expansion and the fear that Germany's powerful steel and coal industries could again provide a basis for aggression.[67] By

65. See "Special Report: Foreign Authorities Expect to Focus on Mergers and Anticartel Law Enforcement," *Antitrust and Trade Regulation Report*, January 30, 1992, pp. 104–05; and (for a more cautious prognosis), "Hungary, Poland Balancing Competition, Need to Protect Firms during Transition," *Antitrust and Trade Regulation Report*, July 9, 1992, pp. 63–64.

66. See Hamburger (1962, pp. 347–77); and Edwards (1964, pp. 61–82).

67. Swann (1970, p. 19).

creating a common and nondiscriminatory market in steel, it was believed, Germany's steelmaking potential would be available to all member nations. Preventing discriminatory access was critical. As a result, the ECSC treaty placed great emphasis on establishing a transparent basing-point system of pricing—a system believed by many economists to impair competition, not to enhance it.[68] The emphasis in the ECSC on maintaining "normal" competition rather than competition per se reflected the belief that competitive conditions in steel had seldom been normal in the past and might not be so in the future. In fact, the ECSC and (later) EC authorities frequently permitted cartels among national producer groups (but not whole common market–spanning cartels), enforced output quotas when supply outraced demand, and approved large horizontal mergers among national producers. Its pro-competitive activities were tempered by a strong concern for stability, the continuity of employment, and the protection of weak producers.[69] Nevertheless, during the first two decades, the most careful analyst of the ECSC's operation found "persistent rivalry and outbreaks of ruthlessly aggressive competition," along with evidence of coordinated market conduct and a reluctance to compete.[70]

The 1957 Treaty of Rome, establishing the much more comprehensive European Economic Community (comprising the six ECSC member nations), was less equivocal in its adoption of pro-competitive measures. The importance of a stronger competition policy was stressed at an early date by an EC commissioner responsible for its implementation:

It is . . . beyond dispute—and the authors of the Treaty were fully aware of this—that it would be useless to bring down trade barriers between Member States if the Governments or private industry were to remain free through economic and fiscal legislation, through subsidies or cartel-like restrictions on competition, virtually to undo the opening of the markets and to prevent, or at least unduly to delay, the action needed to adapt them to the Common Market.[71]

68. For a review of the literature, see Scherer (1980, pp. 325–34).
69. See Edwards (1964, p. 82); Hamburger (1962, pp. 354–57, 364–77); Stegemann (1977).
70. Stegemann (1977, p. 239).
71. Statement of Hans von der Groeben in 1961, quoted in Swann (1970, pp. 53–54). A similar view was expressed by Brittan (1992): "Throughout [the EC experience] it was recognized that competition policy was a necessary complement to the elimination of trade barriers. If, for example, customs duties were replaced by export subsidies or a cartel between companies to divide markets, what would have been achieved? In economic terms, very little. . . . Recently, as the programme to complete the Community's internal market . . . took form and then gathered pace, competition policy has also moved up a gear or two. . . . It now seems to be widely acknowledged that, once the internal market is . . . achieved, the importance of competition policy will be redoubled in order to keep the Community's market open and competitive" (pp. 1–2).

Article 3 of the Treaty of Rome required the "establishment of a system to ensure that competition is not distorted in the Common Market." Article 85 deemed inconsistent with the common market "all agreements between firms . . . and all concerted practices likely to affect trade between Member States," singling out agreements that directly or indirectly fixed prices or other trading terms, limited production or investments, and shared markets.[72] Its reference to "all agreements" had the ring of the per se prohibitions embodied in judicial interpretations of America's Sherman Act. However, article 85 went on to permit exceptions for agreements and concerted practices that contributed "towards improving the production or distribution of goods or promoting technical or economic progress while reserving to users a fair share in the [resulting] profit," provided that the agreements did not go beyond what was essential to attain those objectives, and provided also that competition was not eliminated on "a substantial portion of the products in question." Thus a complex balancing process—what U.S. jurists call a "rule of reason" approach—was instituted. Article 86 prohibited the abuse of a dominant position in the common market or a substantial part thereof, singling out production and marketing limitations, discriminatory pricing and conditions-setting, tying arrangements, and the imposition of "unfair trading terms."

In March 1962 the EC Commission issued regulation 17, setting out procedures for enforcing its competition policy rules. Agreements covered by article 85 of the Rome Treaty were prohibited unless the participants sought an exemption by registering them with the Commission. By 1963, 36,000 agreements had been registered, burying the Commission's staff under an avalanche of paper and hindering initial efforts to identify agreements for which exemption would be denied.[73] Many were cleared away by the issue of block exemptions for presumptively innocuous practices. By 1969 the Commission had taken strong punitive action, including substantial fines, against cartels in quinine and dyestuffs, and enforcement activity escalated thereafter.[74] It was recognized too that some enterprises might attempt to escape the Commission's grasp by keeping their agreements secret, and so the Commission's competition policy directorate began a regular effort to "find and, where necessary, suppress non notified restrictive practices."[75] To carry out this function,

72. U.S. Senate Judiciary Committee (1963, pt. 1, p. 257).
73. U.S. Senate Judiciary Committee (1963, pt. 2, pp. 271–73).
74. Commission of the European Communities (1972, pp. 25–28).
75. Commission of the European Communities (1972, p. 102). Ken George and Alexis Jacquemin speculate that as late as 1980, more than half the agreements prohibited by EC Treaty Article 85 had not been notified to the Commission. George and Jacquemin (1990, p. 220).

it needed the power to discover (that is, seize or subpoena) evidence from recalcitrant cartelists. A setback occurred in 1987 when Hoechst, a chemicals maker, obtained a German court order temporarily barring Commission staff from entering its premises to search for incriminating documents. However, the impasse was broken initially when the German Federal Cartel Office came to the rescue and obtained a search warrant from a Frankfurt court. The Commission imposed fines on Hoechst totaling 55,000 ECUs (European currency units, roughly $75,000), for its delaying tactics—an action validated subsequently by the EC Court of Justice.[76]

How national competition laws with widely varying provisions were to coexist with the competition policy of the European Community was also addressed by the Court of Justice. In a key 1969 decision, the Court ruled that national competition policy authorities could proceed in parallel against questionable practices, but if a conflict materialized, Community law would prevail.[77] The adoption of formal merger control procedures by the EC in 1989 raised new jurisdictional questions. The dividing line between national and Community authority was established in the first instance by setting quantitative thresholds. The 1989 regulation (effective in 1990) gave Commission competition policy authorities primary jurisdiction if the merging enterprises had combined world sales exceeding 5 billion ECUs and sales within the EC of at least 250 million ECUs, but only if the firms had less than two-thirds of their aggregate Community sales in any single member nation. Earlier drafts proposed much lower sales thresholds of 1 billion and 100 million ECUs, but this was opposed by Germany, which feared that its strong merger control program would be undermined.[78] A coordination procedure between the EC and member nations was established. If a national competition policy authority asks to stop a merger technically within the EC's jurisdiction, the EC can refer the merger to that nation for enforcement action, or it can rule that no relevant national market exists. If the EC denies jurisdiction in the latter case, the member nation can appeal to the European Court of Justice for an injunction against the EC's decision.[79] The EC procedures

76. See OECD (1992a, pp. 317–19). Securing information continues to be problematic for EC competition policy authorities. See the summary of an address by Auke Haagsma in "Conferees Address Harmonization of U.S., EC Competition Regimes," *Antitrust and Trade Regulation Report*, October 14, 1993, p. 501.

77. Commission of the European Communities (1972, p. 106).

78. See Schmidt (1992, pp. 112–13); Jacquemin, Buigues, and Ilzkovitz (1989, pp. 68–69); and (on continuation of the higher thresholds) "EC Commission Recommends No Change in Thresholds for Merger Regulation," *Antitrust and Trade Regulation Report*, August 5, 1993, p. 214.

79. Schmidt (1992, pp. 116–17).

appear to centralize merger control power in Brussels somewhat more than the division of responsibilities prevailing between U.S. federal and state antitrust authorities. In the United States, state enforcement officials have been allowed to seek court-ordered divestiture of a merger approved by the Federal Trade Commission.[80]

The European Community law is unique in charging its competition policy directorate (called DG-4) with the task not only of policing restrictive agreements and concentrations of monopoly power but also of combating subsidies (called "state aid") to national (typically, but not always, state-owned) enterprises and preferential national procurement regulations that have the effect of distorting competition within the Community. In effect, competition policy compensates for the elimination within a trading bloc of GATT-authorized countervailing duty imposition procedures when national (or subnational) export subsidies cause injury to the industries of importing nations. Attempts to carry out this mandate have required extremely difficult trade-offs, bringing the EC competition policy directorate into conflict not only with national governments but also with the EC directorate (DG-3) responsible for industrial policy.[81] The privatization of many state-owned European enterprises, partly in response to the EC's 1992 "Single Market" program, was intended, among other goals, to reduce the scope of subsidy and "buy-at-home" distortions. However, state aid to restructure both newly privatized and well-established private enterprises continued at high levels during the early 1990s. Lacking authority to require that state-owned monopolies be broken into smaller competing fragments when they are privatized, the EC competition policy directorate may find that national champion preferences replace the distortions associated with state ownership. Other multinational free trade agreements, such as the North American Free Trade Agreement (NAFTA), have tended to retain GATT-like procedures for combating trade-distorting subsidies and preferences, rather than adding them to the burden carried by competition policy enforcers.

Although there continue to be substantial differences between the competition law of the EC and the laws of individual member nations, the differences have tended to narrow over time as Italy, Spain, and Greece have enacted competition laws for the first time and other mem-

80. *State of California v. American Stores Co. et al.*, 495 U.S. 271 (1990).

81. See Commission of the European Communities (1972, pp. 112–53); George and Jacquemin (1990, pp. 214–19); and "The Single Market Itself Is in Question," *Business Week*, November 1, 1993, p. 52. In late 1991 France challenged before the EC Court of Justice a Commission "communication" requiring state-owned enterprises to file special annual financial reports with the Commission. "France Fires Second Judicial Shot at EC Competition Policy Initiatives," *Antitrust and Trade Regulation Report*, February 20, 1992, p. 14.

bers (such as France) have gradually strengthened their national laws. Also, in the May 1992 treaty under which nations belonging to the European Free Trade Association (EFTA) joined with the EC to form the European Economic Space, it was stipulated at the EC's insistence that the EFTA nations would individually adopt competition policy regimes as strict as those within the Community.[82] Thus the convergence of policies that began following World War II continues.

Efforts to Establish Broader Transnational Policies

Following World War II, the United Nations sought to create international trade coordination mechanisms that would prevent a recurrence of the chaotic conditions of the 1930s. Fifty-seven nations participated in the United Nations Conference on Trade and Employment in Havana, from November 1947 to March 1948. The result was a draft treaty called the Havana Charter, which proposed to create a formal International Trade Organization. One function of the ITO, actually assumed by the GATT organization, would be to promulgate tariff reductions and arbitrate trade barrier and dumping disputes. But in addition, article 46 of the Havana Charter stated:

> Each Member shall take appropriate measures and shall cooperate with the [ITO] to prevent, on the part of private or public commercial enterprises, business practices affecting international trade which restrain competition, limit access to markets, or foster monopolistic control, whenever such practices have harmful effects on the expansion of production or trade and interfere with the achievement of any of the other objectives [of the Charter].[83]

The practices to be prevented were identified to include price-fixing, market division, production quota-setting, discrimination against particular enterprises, collusive suppression of technology, and the misuse of patent grants. The ITO was directed to consult with member nations on alleged violations, urge corrective action, and publish reports on compliance. The Havana Charter failed to elicit a sufficient number of ratifications—most notably from the United States, given senatorial concerns that its broad provisions would infringe too deeply on U.S. sovereignty. Its narrower rules with respect to dumping and trade-distorting subsidies became the basis of GATT in 1948.

82. See Brittan (1992, p. 4).
83. U.S. Department of State (1948, p. 86). The competition policy provisions were anticipated in Mason (1946, pp. 4–5).

Efforts continued under UN auspices, and with U.S. governmental support, to devise an acceptable competition policy that spanned national boundaries. In 1953 a committee comprising delegates from six industrialized nations plus four developing lands (India, Mexico, Pakistan, and Uruguay) produced a United Nations Draft Convention on restrictive practices, which was endorsed by the UN Economic and Social Council and forwarded to UN member nations for ratification.[84] The convention proposed mechanisms to challenge practices affecting international trade that "restrain competition, limit access to markets or foster monopolistic control."[85] The proposed new international agency's secretariat would receive complaints concerning restrictive practices and refer them to its investigative division, leaving to the home nations of accused enterprises the task of collecting evidence and representing the enterprises in a formal hearing. The findings from that hearing would be presented to a Representative Body, in which each signatory nation participated with a single vote per nation. The Representative Body would convey its recommendations to the accused enterprises' home government, letting that nation take "the action *it considers appropriate . . .* and in accordance with its own constitution or system of law and economic organization," recognizing its obligation under the agreement to "take all possible measures" to inhibit restrictive practices within its jurisdiction.[86]

Seven nations endorsed the Draft Convention, but there was strong opposition to it from the U.S. business community, and in the end the United States chose not to ratify it, which frustrated the accumulation of required ratifications from nations accounting for approximately 65 percent of world imports and exports. Opponents emphasized the view that "competitive enterprise as Americans understand it is either forbidden or has never been witnessed by a majority of the 60 nations comprising the U.N."[87] From this, it was argued, implementation would fall discriminatorily heavily upon companies resident in the United States, with its strong antitrust policies. In addition, opponents asserted, the one-signatory one-vote provision would mean that "this UN program will thus stimulate every anticapitalistic participating nation to instigate harassing complaints against the United States and other participating nations whose nationals have the most

84. For a retrospective by the committee's secretary, see Timberg (1973, pp. 157–84).

85. Timberg (1973, p. 170).

86. *Report of the Attorney General's National Committee to Study the Antitrust Laws* (1955, p. 104).

87. *Report of the Attorney General's National Committee to Study the Antitrust Laws* (1955, p. 107). A minority of the Attorney General's Committee favored U.S. ratification. The majority refrained from addressing the issue as outside the scope of its substantive mandate.

extensive world trade, and will so imperil them in their most vital operations."[88] Attempts to formulate a multilateral competition treaty have continued under a variety of formal (such as UN and OECD) and informal auspices, but none has led to an agreement accepted by the community of nations.[89]

Unable to agree on a unified substantive international approach to competition policy, some nations have entered into bilateral cooperation arrangements. There were three discernible waves.

First, Marshall Plan aid agreements reached between the United States and beneficiary nations following World War II contained provisions requiring the coordination of competition policies. There is little evidence that they had significant consequences. Second, the United States entered into numerous bilateral treaties of Friendship, Commerce, and Navigation. They included provisions for mutual consultation with a view to eliminating the harmful effects of restrictive business practices.[90] These too appear to have had little impact. When the defendants in a wire nail cartel case argued that the consultations provided under the FC&N treaty between the United States and Japan provided the only remedy available against Japanese exporters, the defense was rejected.[91]

A third round of bilateral agreements focused explicitly on communication concerning, and coordination of, enforcement actions potentially affecting the subjects of both parties. One of the first was between the United States and West Germany in 1976.[92] Other agreements followed between the United States and Australia (1982), the United States and Canada (1984),[93] France and Germany (1987), and Australia and New Zealand (1990).

88. *Report of the Attorney General's National Committee to Study the Antitrust Laws* (1955). Or as Sigmund Timberg (1973, p. 173) observed prophetically in 1973, "the fear that countries such as Haiti and Iraq would be passing judgment on the performance of U.S. business abroad was one of the factors that finally led to U.S. business antagonism."

89. On the most recent private initiative by twelve lawyers from Germany, the United States, Japan, Switzerland, and Poland, see International Antitrust Code Working Group, "Draft International Antitrust Code as a GATT-MTO-Plurilateral Trade Agreement," Special Supplement, *Antitrust and Trade Regulation Report*, August 19, 1993. It was received with skepticism by an OECD group. "OECD Committee Lacks Enthusiasm for Draft International Antitrust Code," *Antitrust and Trade Regulation Report*, December 16, 1993, pp. 771–72.

90. Timberg (1973, p. 167). Timberg identified ten such treaties as of 1973.

91. *United States* v. *R.P. Oldham Co. et al.*, 152 F. Supp. 818 (1957).

92. "Agreement Relating to Mutual Cooperation Regarding Restrictive Business Practices," 15 I.L.M. (International Legal Materials), p. 1282 (1976).

93. The Canadian agreement evidently replaced an earlier consultative agreement spurred by a dispute between the United States and Canada over a Canadian patent pool that denied licenses to potential U.S. radio and television exporters. See Timberg (1973, pp. 160–61, 167).

In September 1991 the European Community and the United States signed a cooperation agreement.[94] It calls for mutual notification when one party's enforcement activities may affect important interests of the other party; the exchange of information on general policies and specific enforcement actions; assistance by one party in the other's enforcement actions; optional enforcement actions by one party against restraints of trade originating within that party's jurisdiction which adversely affect the welfare of the other party's subjects; and a willingness on both sides "to take into account the important interests of the other Party" and avoid enforcement action conflicts. The agreement does not bind the U.S. and EC authorities to engage in cooperative enforcement; each retains the option to demur. Nevertheless, in December 1991 France filed a complaint with the EC Court of Justice alleging that in entering the agreement, the EC Commission had exceeded its authority.[95] Resolution of the conflict was expected to take approximately two years. Meanwhile, information exchanges between the U.S. agencies and the EC—mostly on recently notified mergers involving U.S. and European companies—continued.[96]

Conclusion

During the past century, there have been dramatic changes in the policies adopted by nations and groups of nations toward monopoly and restrictive practices. Once the United States stood virtually alone in its strong prohibitions against price-fixing and similar restrictive agreements. But there has been a discernible decline in the once-widespread belief that competitive market processes are intrinsically unstable and ruinous. The superiority of competition over cartelization has been acknowledged to an increasing degree, but still not universally. Now most industrialized nations have some kind of competition law, and the European Community has implemented an extensive system of transnational policies. Substantial differences in the details of those policies remain. Some nations follow the United States in prohibiting naked price-fixing rings without qualification; others incline toward letting cartels operate but attempting to control abuses. As is seen more fully in the next

94. "Agreement between the Government of the United States of America and the Commission of the European Communities Regarding the Application of Their Competition Laws," *Antitrust and Trade Regulation Report*, September 26, 1991, pp. 382–85.

95. "France Challenges U.S.-EC Accord in EC Court on Procedural Grounds," *Antitrust and Trade Regulation Report*, January 16, 1992, p. 45.

96. "U.S.-EC Notices Increase since Accord; Confidentiality Concerns Are Downplayed," *Antitrust and Trade Regulation Report*, February 27, 1992, p. 267.

chapter, there are also major differences among national jurisdictions in the extent to which monopoly structures (as distinguished from the exercise of monopoly power) are challenged or inhibited. Such differences have made it difficult but, as the European Community experience demonstrates, not impossible to agree upon competition policies spanning national borders. The two chapters that follow will explore more deeply whether further steps toward the adaptation and coordination of national competition policies are desirable and feasible in an environment of increasingly open international trading relationships.

Chapter 4

Specific Competition Policy Challenges

H AVING laid historical and conceptual foundations, I turn to the specific areas in which competition policy, national trading strategies, and international trade policies have explicitly intersecting interests. This chapter is organized along traditional competition policy target categories, beginning with cartels and other horizontal restraints, and moving on then to dominant positions and mergers that aggrandize them, vertical restraints, price discrimination, and the possibly special challenges posed by multinational enterprises.

Cartels

There are several reasons why individual nations might permit or even encourage cartels and other horizontal agreements with an impact on international trade.

For one, price-fixing or other restrictive agreements among exporting companies may contribute to national industrial policy goals by biasing the terms of trade in the exporting nation's favor and shifting economic rents from importing nations to sellers in the exporting nation.[1] Figure 4-1 illustrates the basic relationships. It assumes a domestic industry with competitive supply curve S facing a foreign demand curve D_{WORLD}. If the industry is left to price competitively, the price will be OP_C and the output OQ_C. By cartelizing, it can derive the foreign market's marginal revenue curve MR, equate S (reflecting marginal cost) with MR, and restrict output to the monopoly level OQ_M, sold at the elevated price

1. See, for example, the discussion of the German Potash Syndicate, in which the German government made participation mandatory after 1910 in order to sustain high prices in the American market. Stolper, Häuser, and Borchardt (1967, p. 48).

Figure 4-1. *Export Monopoly and Equivalent Export Tariff*

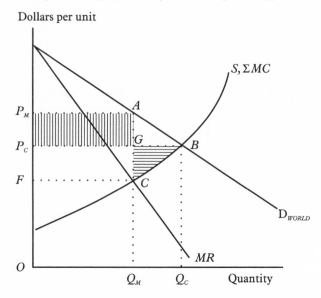

OP_M. By restricting output, the domestic industry sacrifices rents measured by the triangular horizontally shaded area GBC, but more than compensates by gaining the vertically shaded area P_MAGP_C. Thus there is a net gain (captured by suppliers) to the exporting nation from cartelization. A similar result could be achieved without cartelization if the exporting nation's government sets an export tariff of AC per unit of output sold, but this is infrequently observed.[2] Then the rent extracted from foreign consumers P_MAGP_C will be captured by the government as tariff collector, rather than by producers, and in addition rents equal to rectangular area P_CGCF will be transferred from domestic producers to the government.

Domestic producers can also enhance their profits by participating in international cartels with sellers from other nations. A variant common in the 1930s was the spheres of influence cartel, under which, say, Britain's Imperial Chemical Industries agreed with du Pont to refrain from selling in the United States, Central America, and Venezuela, while du Pont ceded the United Kingdom and most British Empire nations (except Canada) to ICI.[3] In Canada and several South American nations, competition was avoided by

2. The export tariff levied during the late 1980s by Canada on its softwood lumber exports is a presumably exceptional example. Forced upon Canada by U.S. efforts to protect timber interests in the United States, it harmed U.S. consumers and apparently enhanced Canadian rents. See Kalt (1988, pp. 339–68).

3. Stocking and Watkins (1946, chaps. 9, 10).

forming joint sales ventures. In addition to facilitating monopoly output (and hence trade volume) restrictions, such cartels distorted what might otherwise have been more complex trade patterns, for example, with both American and British firms selling in the designated areas.

Trading patterns may also be affected by cartel arrangements that ostensibly operate only within the domestic market of firms producing both for domestic consumption and for export. There are two main possibilities. First, firms might reinvest the monopoly profits earned at home in research, development, and capacity expansion, enhancing over time their comparative advantage in export markets. Or second, the production freed up by domestic output restrictions might be "dumped" profitably in export markets. I return to this second case in a subsequent section. For either of these industrial strategies to succeed, it is usually also necessary that the domestic cartel be protected (normally through trade barriers erected by the government) from imports, which might otherwise be attracted by the high domestic prices and undermine them.

Finally, export cartels (often called export associations) might be formed to save selling, financing, and customs paperwork costs by letting a common sales organization handle the transactions of multiple domestic producers, including companies too small to mount their own export campaigns. In this case, both sellers and buyers may gain. To achieve such economies of consolidated selling was the ostensible intent of Congress in passing the first U.S. law authorizing export trading associations, the Webb-Pomerene Act of 1918, and the complementary Export Trading Company Act of 1982.[4] However, there are grounds for doubting whether cost saving has been the main consequence of the Webb-Pomerene and Export Trading Company associations actually formed. The Webb-Pomerene groups have been shown to comprise mainly large firms, not their smaller brethren; and a disproportion have originated in relatively highly concentrated U.S. industries, that is, those in which a few sellers hold substantial market shares.[5] A more recent study of ninety-four export trading companies reveals that only four engaged in foreign government liaison, nine in joint promotion activities, four in the promotion of a U.S. region, four in warranty service, and seven in project coordination.[6] Thirty-seven fixed prices, thirty-six coordinated bids, and fourteen allocated customers.

Most nations explicitly exempt export associations from the prohibitions of their competition policy laws, sometimes (as in the United

4. See Federal Trade Commission (1967, pp. 2–6); and Davidow (1983, pp. 358–59).

5. Federal Trade Commission (1967, chaps. 3, 4). For similar findings on Japanese export cartels, see Jacquemin and others (1981).

6. OECD (1993b, p. 29).

States) insisting that competition-reducing spillover effects be avoided in domestic markets, sometimes not. To permit regulatory oversight, registration of an association seeking exemption, and disclosure of its functions, are often required.[7]

The Extent of Cartelization

It is perhaps surprising that despite their cost-saving and price-raising potential, formally registered export trade associations appear to originate only small fractions of national exports. At their peak during the early 1930s, U.S. Webb-Pomerene associations handled approximately 19 percent of U.S. exports.[8] By 1981 only thirty-nine Webb-Pomerene associations, accounting for less than 2 percent of U.S. exports, remained active.[9] In West Germany, sixty export cartels alleged not to have effects in the domestic market and four conceding domestic effects were registered as of 1980. Their share of German exports has been estimated at 2 percent.[10] The average number of exempted Japanese export cartels was 202 between 1964 and 1973, with a slight downward trend.[11] Roughly half of the registered Japanese export cartels during the early 1980s were from a single industry, textiles.[12]

The amount of cartelized trade—including sub rosa activity not registered with national authorities—appears to have dropped considerably since the 1930s, when, it is estimated very crudely, from 30 to 50 percent of world trade was subjected to some degree of cartel control.[13] The decline is probably attributable in significant measure to the increasingly hostile legal environment.

International Cartel Law and Its Enforcement

Legal developments have in some respects inhibited and in others facilitated the cartelization of world trading activity. Much depends upon the specific form of cartel organization and the degree of government involvement. Four main categories are usefully distinguished: cross-border cartels

7. See, for example, OECD (1984, pp. 33–34); and American Bar Association (1991, pp. 40–73).

8. OECD (1984, p. 30).

9. OECD (1984, p. 30).

10. OECD (1984, p. 30); Audretsch (1989, p. 591).

11. Fair Trade Commission (1973, p. 27).

12. OECD (1984, p. 30).

13. Mason (1946, p. 26); Davidow (1983, p. 351). Mason hastens to add his opinion that "the injury inflicted by tariffs on domestic competition and American foreign trade has been several times greater than the effect of cartels" (p. 28).

among nationalized enterprises; cross-border cartels among private entities; export cartels operating from a single country; and restrictive arrangements such as voluntary restraint agreements and orderly marketing agreements formed to resolve international trade policy conflicts.

The most influential cartel in modern world history is the Organization of Petroleum Exporting Countries. OPEC is a cartel of national governments' oil-owning authorities. Its successful effort to raise crude oil prices from $3 to $12 a barrel in early 1974 drained approximately $90 billion from oil-consuming nations and, because the funds could not be respent quickly on imports, contributed to a worldwide recession. Further OPEC-induced price increases to more than $30 per barrel in the late 1970s, combined with central bank efforts to combat the lingering inflation from earlier price shocks, precipitated a second wave of worldwide recessions between 1980 and 1983.

In December 1978 a labor union, the International Association of Machinists and Aerospace Workers, attempted to use the U.S. antitrust laws to enjoin OPEC's price-raising activities and obtain monetary damages for the harm done. After extensive testimony, the suit was dismissed.[14] The principal initial basis for dismissal was that sovereign foreign nations are immune from the jurisdiction of U.S. federal courts:

> It is clear that the nature of the activity engaged in by each of these OPEC member countries is the establishment by a sovereign state of the terms and conditions for the removal of a prime natural resource, to wit, crude oil from its territory.[15]

Endorsing this line of argument but emphasizing another, the court of appeals concluded that OPEC's conduct constituted "acts of state," posing politically sensitive international relations issues properly decided upon under the U.S. constitutional separation of powers by the president and Congress, and not by the judiciary:

> When the courts engage in piecemeal adjudication of the legality of the sovereign acts of states, they risk disruption of our country's international diplomacy. . . . The possibility of insult to the OPEC states and of interference with the efforts of the political branches to seek favorable relations with them is apparent from the very nature of this action and the remedy sought.[16]

14. *International Association of Machinists and Aerospace Workers* v. *The Organization of Petroleum Exporting Countries*, 477 F. Supp. 553 (1979); 649 F. 2d 1354 (1981).
15. 477 F. Supp. 567.
16. 649 F. 2d 1358, 1361. See also *Hartford Fire Insurance Co.* v. *California*, 113 S. Ct. 2891 (June 1993).

The act of state doctrine also limits the vulnerability of international cartels among private enterprises and single-nation private firm export cartels to the competition laws of a nation whose consumers are adversely affected. Fine distinctions have emerged.[17] If cartelization occurs under active compulsion from the government of the colluding firms' domicile, it is likely to be exempt from other nations' reach. If, however, the cartel operates without the knowledge of the host nation, or if it is registered with the host nation's government but not actively mandated by that government, and if its main *effects* occur in the jurisdiction from which a legal action is pursued (the "effects" doctrine), it may not escape censure under "act of state" claims.[18]

In a key case, the European Community successfully prosecuted an international cartel of wood pulp suppliers to the EC, including (along with Scandinavian companies) a group of U.S. firms registered as an export cartel under the Webb-Pomerene Act. The U.S. cartel members insisted that because Webb-Pomerene associations were considered by the United States to be beneficial to its economy, the Community should not interfere with them. This defense was rejected by the EC Court of Justice, asserting that Webb-Pomerene associations are merely *allowed*, and not *required*, by U.S. law, and therefore the act of state noninterference principle did not hold.[19] The U.S. Department of Justice, which in the past had sued to enjoin the activities of registered foreign export cartels under similar doctrinal interpretations, stated after consultation with EC competition policy officials that it would voice no objections to the EC's wood pulp initiative.[20]

More generally, an OECD committee observed that "countries are increasingly less likely to defer to the policies of their trading partners of granting exemption to export cartels."[21] However, some nations—notably, the United Kingdom, Canada, Australia, and France—have taken strong exception to U.S. efforts to exercise jurisdiction over collusive activities by their nationals under the "effects" doctrine.[22] Among other things, they have enacted laws that make it difficult to subpoena evidence

17. See American Bar Association (1991, chaps. 5, 6); and U.S. Department of Justice, "Antitrust Guidelines for International Operations," 53 Fed. Reg. 21595–97 (1988). I have benefited greatly on this point from Rabinowitz (1993).

18. On the early cases, see Timberg (1973, pp. 158–61). Timberg comments that the exercise by the U.S. courts of "ever-increasing jurisdiction over non-U.S. firms . . . produced a large number of diplomatic tensions and protests" (p. 160).

19. *A. Åhlström Osakeyhtiö et al.* v. *Commission of the European Communities,* 1988 E.C.R. 5193 (1988).

20. Rabinowitz (1993, p. 29).

21. OECD (1984, p. 36).

22. For the "If you can't beat 'em, join 'em" file, see "Canadian Court Fines Japanese Firm $900,000 for Anticompetitive Conspiracy," *Antitrust and Trade Regulation Report,* November 25, 1993, pp. 691–92.

or otherwise elicit the cooperation of cartel members in their home jurisdictions.[23]

Cartels whose participants are private companies from a diversity of nations may seek exemption from the competition policy actions of an affected nation under the act-of-state doctrine. In such cases, however, national litigation against the cartels can often disrupt or deter, since some members are likely to have their headquarters in a country with strong anticartel policies. And the absence of key players from nations like the United States may be sufficient to render the cartel ineffective, even if other firms' governments lend their active assent. Numerous antitrust actions by the United States against U.S. companies involved during the 1930s and 1940s in international cartels with adverse effects on the U.S. market were instrumental in deterring further participation, and the resulting absence of the U.S. firms has almost surely been a major reason why cross-border cartels have dwindled in number and significance.[24] Nevertheless, parent company residence in a strong antitrust jurisdiction may be insufficient to bar cartel activity. A Canadian subsidiary of Gulf Oil Corporation was at least urged and possibly compelled by the Canadian government to participate in a worldwide cartel of uranium producers during the early 1970s.[25] Protests against U.S. efforts to exercise jurisdiction were filed by Canada, Australia, and the United Kingdom. These, and especially the Canadian intervention, evidently influenced the Department of Justice to settle its case against Gulf with a small fine rather than bringing felony charges, as Justice staff initially recommended.[26] On the other hand, when the various competition policy jurisdictions cooperate, efforts to inhibit cartelization can be especially potent. For instance, the European Community and the United States pursued separate but parallel actions against an international quinine cartel, in each case levying substantial fines against the companies involved.[27]

International trade policy and competition policy come into acute substantive, though not procedural, conflict when the government of one nation asks the government of another nation to have its producers voluntarily restrain their exports because the exports are believed to be dumped, subsidized, or otherwise materially injurious to the importing nation's industry. Such VRAs (voluntary restraint agreements), also called VERs (voluntary export restraints), proliferated during the 1970s and

23. Rabinowitz (1993, p. 29); Timberg (1973, pp. 180–81).
24. On the cartels' various modes of operation, see, for example, Berge (1944); Stocking and Watkins (1946); and Stocking and Watkins (1948).
25. See Mirow and Maurer (1982, pp. 106–10).
26. Mirow and Maurer (1982, pp. 116–18).
27. Davidow (1983, p. 365).

Figure 4-2. *Import Restraint through Tariff and Equivalent Quota*

Dollars per unit

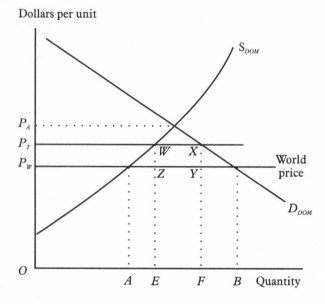

1980s, with the European Community and the United States as the most active instigators.[28] Janusz Ordover and Linda Goldberg report that more than a third of Japan's exports to the United States and the EC in recent years have been covered by such restraints.

Figure 4-2 suggests why they are a popular way of dealing with international trade disputes. Let S_{DOM} be the supply curve of a nation's domestic producers and D_{DOM} the domestic demand function. If the market were served autarkically—that is, without imports—the competitive price would be OP_A. Suppose (oversimplifying) that the consuming nation's demand for imports is sufficiently small relative to world supply that imports can be obtained at the constant (competitive) world price OP_W. Then the domestic price will be competed down to OP_W, domestic firms will supply quantity OA, and importers will supply quantity AB. Suppose now that this large volume of imports and the resulting low price are considered by national trade policy authorities to be injurious to the domestic industry. If the requisite GATT conditions can be satisfied, the situation could be rectified by imposing a tariff per unit of $P_T P_W$, raising the price to OP_T, reducing the quantity of exports to EF, and increasing the quantity supplied by domestic firms to OE. The amount of tariff revenue realized by the importing nation's treasury is given by the rectangle $WXYZ$. An identical increase in prices and domestic firm

28. OECD (1993b, pp. 25–26).

output could be achieved by fixing an import quota or, more to the point, having other nations' exporters agree to limit their shipments to the quantity EF. There is, however, a major difference. Under a quota system, voluntary or mandatory, the surplus of domestic price realizations over the world price $P_T P_W$ accrues to the exporting nations' producers, and not to the importing nation's tariff collector. Thus exporters capture rents of $WXYZ$ that they would not receive from selling at the competitive world price *or* from having a special tariff levied on their goods. To be sure, they lose export volume relative to the no-tariff situation, but they are much better off under a VRA than they would be under an equivalently import-limiting tariff. This is why they "volunteer" to maintain the restrictions.

Why the importing nation prefers a VRA over the revenues it could gain through an added tariff is more subtle. The main explanation is that VRAs minimize international friction. The other nations' producers refrain from filing troublesome and embarrassing complaints with GATT alleging breaches of most-favored-nation treatment.[29] The principal losers are the importing nation's consumers, who would lose in any event (even though their tax bills might be reduced because of enhanced tariff revenues). However, VRAs are inflexible instruments, inhibiting desirable changes in the import volume to shifts in domestic demand or world supply (and hence the world price of the imported good). Also, if the domestic industry is monopolistic rather than competitive, as assumed so far, VRA quotas may induce greater domestic price increases than do tariffs eliciting the same restriction of output.[30] Thus they may also be favored by competing producers in the importing nation.[31] The more severe home-market price effects and efficiency sacrifices accepted with VRA quotas than with equivalent tariffs suggest that minimizing trading partner anger is indeed the principal motivation for the frequent choice of VRAs.

When quotas are negotiated, they must be divided among the various producers of the exporting nation. One way to do so is for the government of the exporting nation to auction off the quotas to the highest bidders. This is done in Hong Kong, for example, to allocate textile and clothing export quotas under the International Multifiber Arrangement.

---

29. However, if VRAs attempt to avoid arbitrage by limiting exports to nations not party to the agreement, international conflict may be provoked. Thus the European Community complained to GATT when Japan agreed with the United States in 1986 to set minimum cost-based prices on *all* dynamic random-access memory chip exports, and not merely on those exported to the United States. In March 1988 a GATT panel ruled that the third party restraints were illegal. See Flamm (forthcoming).

30. See OECD (1984, pp. 96–101); and OECD (1993b, pp. 31–44).

31. For an analysis concluding that high tariffs might have been preferred over VRAs by importing nation producers, see Messerlin (1989b).

Then the government of the exporting nation, rather than its producers, receives most if not all of the quota rent *WXYZ* in figure 4-2. But more commonly, the problem is solved by forming a de facto cartel among the quota-holding nation's producers, requiring each to limit its exports to its assigned share of the national quota.

Since a certain amount of interfirm coordination is required, if only to ensure that individual firm outputs add up to the quota total, such arrangements effected for international trade policy reasons might run afoul of importing nation laws that seek to discourage restrictive practices by exporting nation firms. Indeed, in the United States, the Consumers Union brought a law suit challenging the voluntary export restraints adopted in 1969 by Japanese and European steel producers under pressure from the U.S. government. A federal district court questioned the legality of the restraints under the Sherman Act, but an appellate court found (with one judge dissenting) that negotiating such restraints was within the U.S. president's foreign policy powers. The court's decision left unsettled the question whether the foreign steelmakers might under some circumstances be held liable for antitrust violations.[32] To avoid such embarrassing imbroglios, the U.S. government took elaborate precautions in 1981 and 1982 to ensure that the Japanese government "compelled" "voluntary" export restraints to the United States by Japanese auto manufacturers.[33]

Exemptions from Cartel Prohibitions

Most national competition laws exempt from their cartel prohibitions certain cooperative activities considered prima facie desirable. The United States, for instance, exempts most export cartels, agricultural cooperatives, cooperative research and development arrangements, insurance company rate-setting activities, baseball player assignments (at least, thus far), and labor union collective bargaining efforts from the Sherman Act's authority. Other gray-area practices that are not restrictive on their face are subjected to a "rule of reason" analysis. Other nations' competition laws tend to authorize a wider array of exemptions. German law allows

32. *Consumers Union of U.S., Inc.*, v. *William Rogers et al.*, 352 F. Supp. 1319 (1973); vacated on appeal in *Consumers Union of U.S., Inc.* v. *Henry Kissinger et al.*, 506 F. 2d 136 (1974), cert. den. 421 U.S. 1004 (1975).

33. This playacting was required in part because the Reagan administration, having promised not to be protectionist, wanted to avoid the onus of openly requesting VRAs from Japan. Rabinowitz (1993, p. 55, n. 156); Davidow (1983, pp. 371–75).

In 1993 an advisory committee to the Japanese Fair Trade Commission cautioned that VRAs had unfavorable competitive effects in both the importing and exporting nations. *Nihon Keizai Shinbun,* June 29, 1993.

exemptions under certain circumstances for "crisis" (that is, recession) cartels, rationalization and specialization cartels (such as closing plants and reassigning production orders to improve efficiency), export and import cartels, and "conditions" cartels (setting uniform terms for delivery and invoice payment).[34] Japan provides exemptions under specified conditions for depression cartels, rationalization cartels, small and medium-size enterprise cartels, and certain regulated industry activities, along with export and import cartels and cartels organized under explicit statutory mandates.[35] In late 1993 the Japanese Fair Trade Commission proposed that such exemptions be abolished by the end of 1995.[36] Whether the recommendation will be accepted remains uncertain. The European Community temporarily exempted some industries, notably synthetic fibers, shipbuilding, and steel, from cartel prohibitions in order to wring out excess capacity.[37] The United States undertook a massive program of cartelization under the National Industrial Recovery Act of 1933 in an effort to "reflate" the economy from severe depression by raising prices and wages, but the government lurched back to procompetitivepolicies in 1935, when the cartel approach was perceived to make matters worse, not better.[38]

34. Audretsch (1989). Rationalization and specialization cartels are permitted only if they are expected to reduce costs and prices, but Audretsch shows through a statistical analysis that prices in industries with such cartels tended to rise at above-average rates (pp. 594–99). On Canada's adoption of specialization cartels to mitigate the problem of uneconomically small production lots and the analogous EC experience, see Stegemann (1979, pp. 449–86).

35. Fair Trade Commission (1973). Ostensibly domestic cartels might have international trade ramifications. For example, the sharp 1973–74 increase in oil and hence electricity prices made domestically smelted aluminum uneconomic in Japan. A special cartel was authorized to coordinate large capacity reductions. Japanese primary aluminum producers were exempted from the 9.3 percent import tariff up to the quantity of aluminum capacity to be closed. They imported ingots from plants they had established in low-electricity-cost nations and paid the tariff savings to an industry association, which in turn used the money to subsidize domestic plant closures. This arrangement gave them a strategic advantage over foreign aluminum sources during the transitional period. See Peck, Levin, and Goto (1988, pp. 224–25).

36. "JFTC Expects to Propose Elimination of Cartels Now Exempt from Antitrust Attack," *Antitrust and Trade Regulation Report*, November 4, 1993, pp. 604–05.

37. See, for example, Shaw and Shaw (1983); "The Common Market's Rush into Cartels," *Business Week*, March 27, 1978, pp. 107–08; and W. Schlieder, "Competition within the EC" (letter to the editor), *Business Week*, May 15, 1978, p. 4. The EC reversed its June 1977 synthetic fiber cartel approval decision in November 1978.

38. See Hawley (1966). A 1933 Supreme Court decision approved a coal industry cartel attempting to cope with "deplorable" economic conditions, but the decision was an anomaly, replaced in 1940 by a return to consistent per se prohibition of horizontal price-fixing and output-allocating agreements. Compare *Appalachian Coals, Inc., et al.* v. *United States*, 288 U.S. 344 (1933); with *United States* v. *Socony-Vacuum Oil Co. et al.*, 310 U.S. 150 (1940).

Proposals for international competition policy treaties during the 1940s recognized that systematic exceptions might be desirable or politically necessary, or both. Edward S. Mason, for example, would have exempted from his proposed pro-competitive international rules government-managed price agreements covering basic agricultural commodities and perhaps also such raw minerals as copper and tin, because "output responds slowly to increased prices, but once expanded it is extremely difficult to contract," because resources are immobile, because workers' income depends directly on prices, and because a large number of workers are employed.[39] The draft Havana Charter made provision for intergovernmental agreements to set and stabilize the prices of "primary commodities," defined as "any product of farm, forest, or fishery or any mineral" in its natural or preliminarily processed form.[40] Such agreements would be permitted only when an official determination was made that

> (a) a burdensome surplus . . . has developed or is expected to develop, which . . . would cause serious hardship to producers among whom are small producers who account for a substantial portion of the total output, and that these conditions could not be corrected by normal market forces in time to prevent such hardship, because, characteristically . . . a substantial reduction in price does not readily lead to a significant increase in consumption or to a significant decrease in production; or
> (b) widespread unemployment or under-employment . . . has developed or is expected to develop, which, in the absence of specific governmental action, would not be corrected by normal market forces in time to prevent widespread and undue hardship to workers.[41]

It seems unlikely that the OPEC cartel could satisfy these criteria, among other things, because there are virtually no small producers and because, given the possibilities of conserving crude oil for future sale, long-run profit-maximizing producers would reduce their output in response to a substantial temporary price decrease.

Import Cartels

Many nations exempt import (or purchasers') cartels under competition policy criteria similar to those for export cartels. However, the incidence of import cartels appears to be much lower. In Japan, for example,

---

39. Mason (1946, pp. 36–37, 141–42). On the possibility of aggregate welfare increases under buffer stock cartels that store output during recession for sale when business recovers, see Scherer and Ross (1990, pp. 298–306).

40. U.S. Department of State (1948, p. 92).

41. U.S. Department of State (1948, p. 97).

Figure 4-3. *Domestic Monopsony and Equivalent Import Tariff*

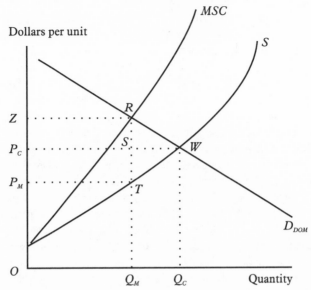

there were on average 202 exempted export cartels functioning between the years 1964 and 1973, but fewer than 3 (on average) import cartels.[42] In West Germany between 1973 and 1983, no import cartels were approved, while the number of approved export cartels in force averaged 65.[43]

There are various reasons why nations might sanction import cartels. One standard case is illustrated in figure 4-3. A nation's demand curve for some commodity available mainly from overseas sources is D_{DOM}. The nation is assumed to be a sufficiently important purchaser of the commodity for the prices charged by competitive suppliers to rise with increased import volume; that is, the supply curve S is upward sloping. If competitive market forces are allowed to operate, the purchase price will be OP_C and the quantity OQ_C. If the importing nation organizes purchasers of the commodity into a buying cartel, the cartel will have monopsony power and, taking into account the effect of its purchases on price, will compute the marginal supply cost MSC of diverse quantities purchased. Then the cartel will restrict its purchases until the marginal supply cost has fallen into equality with the marginal value of the commodity, read off the demand curve at point R. The quantity purchased will be OQ_M, which the importers will be willing to supply at the price OP_M—consid-

42. Fair Trade Commission (1973, p. 27).
43. Audretsch (1989, p. 591).

erably less than the competitive price OP_C. The buying cartel gains at the expense of suppliers the monopsony rent P_CSTP_M, sacrificing a much smaller triangular surplus RWS because of its output restriction. As with a sellers' cartel, the same outcome can be achieved if the buying nation imposes an appropriate tariff—in this case of ZP_M per unit imported. Then the government as tariff collector will capture the monopsony rent P_CSTP_M and also transfer to itself $ZRSP_C$, which would have been buying firms' surplus under either competitive or monopsony purchasing.

Since there are plausible reasons why nations might want import cartels, the rarity of such cartels seems puzzling. There are at least four possible explanations. Some might not be reported to avoid putting exporting industries on notice. Finance ministers may prefer tariffs to letting their domestic companies appropriate the rents from exporters. Domestic firms may have difficulty mustering significant monopsony power vis-à-vis exporters. Or exporters may be able to circumvent the cartels (as they also avoid tariffs) by setting up their own production facilities in the importing nations. The relative explanatory power of these hypotheses remains unknown.

Many economists' advocacy of stiff import tariffs on imported crude oil follows in part the rationale of figure 4-3. If OPEC's supply curve for oil is upward sloping—for example, because the oil-producing nations' ability to avoid chiseling on their price agreements is weakened when quantities demanded are restricted and there is much excess capacity—demand-curbing tariffs might keep crude petroleum prices lower than they otherwise would be.

Because OPEC is a sellers' cartel, buying nations may take countermeasures not merely to exploit its upward-sloping supply function, following the logic of figure 4-3, but also to thwart the price-raising efforts of monopolistic foreign suppliers. That rationale was explicit in the 1971 decision by the U.S. government to exempt American petroleum companies from antitrust prosecution so that they could negotiate collectively in Teheran against Persian Gulf nations' price increase demands.[44] The attempt was unsuccessful. One of the first agreements allowed by the British Restrictive Practices Court to pass through an exemption "gateway" was an import cartel by sulfuric acid manufacturers to countervail an export cartel registered by U.S. sulfur producers under the Webb-Pomerene Act.[45] Similarly, a Japanese buyers' cartel was formed to countervail an international cartel of wood chip suppliers, including a U.S. Webb-Pomerene export association. The Webb-Pomerene group responded by suing under U.S. antitrust law to enjoin

44. U.S. Senate Foreign Relations Committee (1975, pp. 127–33). See also OECD (1984, p. 42).

45. *In re National Sulfuric Acid Association's Agreement,* 4 R.P. 169 (1963).

what it alleged to be a Japanese boycott against its exports. A U.S. court assumed extraterritorial jurisdiction and ruled in favor of the American wood chip exporters.[46] Whether the ruling increased the exporters' Japanese market access is unknown.

Another asserted rationale for buyers' cartels is to limit or keep imports out when they might otherwise compete with domestically produced goods. It is unclear why *buyers* would wish to accomplish this unless they were also vertically integrated into the production of the commodity they were buying. This appears to have been the situation of the Japanese soda ash import cartel, whose only members were the four manufacturers of soda ash in Japan. The cartel was ordered by the Japanese Fair Trade Commission in 1983 to cease its import restrictions.[47] The complex economic motives observed in such cases overlap those present in other kinds of restrictions involving vertical market relationships, to be analyzed in a later section.

International Technology-Sharing Agreements

Agreements to license patents and technological know-how pose peculiarly difficult competition policy trade-offs. On the one hand, the licenses may include agreements to divide among the participating companies product assignments or exclusive geographic territories, to allocate production quotas within a market, or to fix the prices of patented products—restrictions that, absent the patent complication, would normally be prohibited under any reasonably tough competition law. Writing in 1946, Edward S. Mason estimated that nine-tenths of the international cartels in which American firms participated took such patent-related forms.[48] On the other hand, production is likely to be more efficient, and product quality higher, when companies can use other firms' complementary technology as well as their own. Also, the rewards to technological innovation may be greater, and hence incentives to conduct R&D stronger, when patent holders can derive benefits from licensing their patents on favorable terms to others. For them to refrain from licensing, exploiting their inventions alone, as the logic of the patent

46. *Daishowa International* v. *North Coast Export Co. et al.*, CCH 1982–2 Trade Cases, para. 64,774 (1982). Similarly, the Department of Justice brought an action against a Japanese import cartel that sought to fix the prices of Alaskan crabs and other seafood. *United States* v. *C. Itoh & Co. et al.*, CCH 1982–83 Trade Cases, Para. 65,010 (1982).

47. OECD (1984, p. 41). Soda ash is used mainly to produce glass. More recently, Japanese glassmakers allegedly exerted pressure on their captive distributors to prevent them from buying flat glass from the United States. See "Commerce Cops," *Business Week,* December 13, 1993, pp. 69–70.

48. Mason (1946, p. 49).

grant clearly permits, might be a decidedly second-best solution. Addressing the trade-off, Mason concluded pessimistically:

> There is little likelihood . . . when two firms have pooled their research facilities and results as closely as have du Pont and ICI, that substantial competition can be restored between them by any sort of governmental action, national or international. Public policy is pretty much faced with a choice of accepting, along with the technological interchange, a substantial diminution of competition, or of attempting to preserve competition by denying the right to exchange technology. It is the author's view that the advantages of the interchange heavily outweigh the unavoidable restraints involved.[49]

In the first two sentences of this judgment Mason, the founder of the Harvard school of industrial organization analysis, was almost surely wrong. The U.S. government did try to restore substantial competition by vigorously attacking the many international cartels organized around patent licenses. To pursue the example offered by Mason, England's Imperial Chemical Industries and du Pont had extensive patent cross-licensing-agreements under which they agreed to stay out of each other's home and imperial markets and use ICI marketing channels in other nations.[50] When the government brought antitrust charges, du Pont canceled its formal agreements. But the government persisted and won its case.[51] The joint marketing arrangements were enjoined, and both companies were required to license a substantial number of patents—including the patents on nylon and polyethylene—to all applicants at "reasonable" royalties.[52] Du Pont established its own production and marketing facilities in Canada and South America, and the two companies began to compete independently in those markets. Several additional chemical makers took advantage of the patent licenses to begin producing synthetic plastics and fibers in the United States. Competition increased markedly.[53] Technology exchanges and patent cross-licensing continued, although under less restrictive conditions. There is no evidence that the government's attack on the restrictive use of patents in chemicals and many other industries led to a significant diminution of incentives for R&D investment.[54]

49. Mason (1946, p. 53).
50. See Whitney (1958, vol. 1, pp. 212–17); and Stocking and Watkins (1946, chaps. 9–11).
51. *United States* v. *Imperial Chemical Industries, Ltd., et al.,* 100 F. Supp. 504 (1951), 105 F. Supp. 215 (1952).
52. ICI, however, secured a British court order preventing the licensing of its patents within the United Kingdom.
53. Whitney (1958, pp. 214–17).
54. See Scherer (1977, pp. 50–78).

Although the formal case law remains unsettled and confusing, the U.S. government's successes in attacking spheres of influence, market sharing, and other restrictions in patent cross licenses put companies on warning that they bore serious risks of antitrust prosecution if they attempted to orchestrate substantial international market restraints around their collective patent holdings.[55] However, scholars began to criticize the government's hard-line policy.[56] A key assumption in their analyses was that the expectation of monopoly rewards through the exercise of patent rights is the principal incentive for investment in research and development (R&D). Thus restrictions imposed in licensing those rights to others enhance the expected rewards from innovation, and hence are unambiguously desirable. Ignored in the analyses was a substantial trove of evidence showing that in most industries the exploitation of patent protection is a relatively unimportant incentive for innovation. Far more important on average are first-mover advantages interacting with the high cost of duplication and the pressure of competition.[57] The critics nevertheless won the hearts and minds of the Reagan administration's Department of Justice. In 1988 new international antitrust guidelines announced a more sympathetic "rule of reason" view toward patent license restrictions intended mainly "to appropriate the inherent value of the technology" unless the restrictions were "part of a sham licensing scheme disguising a naked cartel."[58] Restrictions that had their impact only outside the United States market would not be attacked. Whether that policy will persist under a new administration remains uncertain.[59] Given the history of policy swerves, companies entering cross licenses with their overseas rivals are well advised to exercise restraint in implementing restraints.

When command over the most up-to-date technology is diffused among numerous companies in several industrialized nations, and when international cartel restrictions are discouraged by the competition laws of one or more nations, newcomers to a field seldom experience difficulty obtaining access to the necessary patent licenses and know-how. Yet exceptions may arise. For example, South Korea moved to the technological frontier in steelmaking by licensing technology from Japanese

55. *Unilateral* restraints—for example, when patent holder A licenses firm B to use its patents, but only on certain products sold in restricted geographic areas—remained clearly within the U.S. law's bounds, although unilaterally imposed price-setting hovered in a gray area owing to two Supreme Court cases "hung" on 4–4 divisions.

56. See especially Bowman (1973); and Andewelt (1984). Compare Kaplow (1984).

57. See Mansfield (1986); and Levin and others (1987).

58. 53 Fed. Reg. 21594 (1988).

59. See "Bingaman Details Division Priorities in International Antitrust Enforcement," *Antitrust and Trade Regulation Reporter,* October 28, 1993, p. 568.

companies. When the Pohang Iron and Steel Company became one of the world's most efficient producers and began shipping large quantities of steel to Japan, "Japanese steel makers [became] increasingly reluctant to transfer know-how to their erstwhile student."[60] Similar developments have been reported in the integrated circuit field. How multiple technology transfer sources suddenly go dry when competition intensifies is not altogether clear. It is also unclear whether there is a significant problem, since other nations' steel (for example, from Europe) and semiconductor specialists appear to have been willing to fill the gap. Nevertheless, the phenomenon is one that bears watching by those with an interest in international competition policy.

The goals of competition policy might also conflict with achieving rapid technological progress when rival companies form joint ventures to develop a new product or process.[61] Most industrialized nations, including the United States with its National Cooperative Research and Development Act of 1984, have exempted such cooperation within broadly defined bounds from competition law prohibitions. In 1993 the exemption was extended to joint production of new products. When the cooperative agreements place few restraints on the postdevelopment commercialization of innovations, leave entry into the consortium open, require postdevelopment licensing, and do not preclude independent initiatives, they pose at worst mild threats to competition policy goals. Nonetheless, difficult cases can arise. An example is the collaboration proposed in 1993 between Boeing and members of Europe's Airbus Industrie group, which together originate three-fourths of world airliner production, to develop an 800-passenger superjumbo.[62] The costs of developing such an aircraft are so huge and the learning-by-doing economies so pervasive that it would be foolhardy for the project to be replicated by two competitors. But joint development lessens competitive pressures to innovate,[63] and joint marketing facilitates setting prices that hold an umbrella over the smaller aircraft sold independently by the two firms. Also, on less massive projects pursuing poorly explored technological avenues, progress is apt to be more rapid, and higher-quality solu-

---

60. Amsden (1989, p. 309).

61. See the symposium on "Collaboration, Innovation and Antitrust" (1990); and Scott (1993, chap. 12).

62. "Now for the Really Big One," *The Economist*, January 9, 1993, pp. 57–58.

63. An egregious case was the joint project on pollution control devices by the principal U.S. automobile manufacturers, who shared little enthusiasm about introducing the costly devices for which governmental regulators were clamoring. The result was a concerted but in the end unsuccessful effort to stall technological progress. See the U.S. Department of Justice confidential memorandum reproduced in "Smog Control Antitrust Case," *Congressional Record*, May 18, 1971, pp. 15626–37.

tions are likely, when multiple independent centers of technological initiative are maintained, especially when the potential market is large relative to R&D costs.[64]

Market Structure, Market Dominance, and Mergers

Competition policy measures directed toward cartels and other restrictive agreements attempt to channel the *conduct* of market participants in rivalrous directions. A quite different approach is for nations to target enforcement toward *market structure*, intervening surgically to maintain enough sellers for competitive conduct to occur more or less automatically. Structural policy is implemented in two main ways: by breaking up consolidations of monopoly power when they have coalesced, and by attempting to prevent such consolidations in their incipiency, notably through merger controls.

Proposals to control market structures raise particularly difficult conflicts between competition policy and industrial policy. One major goal of nations' industrial policies is to build enterprises sufficiently large to achieve all economies of scale, both static (that is, in production and marketing) and dynamic (for example, in carrying out technological innovations). If a national market is small, it may be difficult to accommodate enough firms to ensure vigorous competition and at the same time to take full advantage of scale economies. The fear of scale economy losses is said to have been a deterrent to structural fragmentation measures in small nations such as Sweden and Canada and even in France.[65] With an extraordinarily large internal market, the United States was typically able to have its cake and eat it, which may explain why it led the way toward policies curbing structural monopolies and mergers.

The reduction of international trade barriers following the implementation of GATT might, in principle, have eased this concern, letting sellers view the world, and not just the boundaries of a single nation, as their market. This was plainly the approach adopted by the most rapidly growing companies in the Japanese steel, auto, consumer electronics, and semiconductor industries. However, to see one's opportunities the way the Japanese saw them requires attitudes that were less than fully developed in Europe. A statistical analysis reveals that strong export sales contribute

64. See Klein (1977); Nelson (1961); and Scherer (1966).
65. See, for example, Hjalmarsson (1992, pp. 337–43), who notes that in Sweden the industrial policy emphasis on structural rationalization has led to reliance on competition from abroad as a substitute for domestic competition policy; Waverman (1990, p. 75); and Jenny (1990, pp. 147, 184).

significantly to the realization of larger plant sizes, other things being equal.[66] However, European enterprises appeared to be more constrained in their plant scale choices by their home market shares and the size of their home markets than were U.S. and Canadian firms. This led me to speculate:

> What may be operating in Europe is a set of self-fulfilling expectations: If producers believe they need a large market share to build large plants, concentration will in fact be an important contributor to efficiency. Alternatively, the spirit of oligopolistic interdependence and respect for established market shares may simply be stronger in Europe. In the more individualistic North American business environment, producers may be more inclined to struggle, among other things through price competition, to realize scale economies, and concentration assumes a less important (though not vanishing) role.[67]

Structural Fragmentation

It is clear that the worldwide reduction of tariff barriers and the even more dramatic unification of the European common market have not eliminated the EC member nations' fear that a strongly pro-competitive structural policy could thwart the realization of scale economies and impair European firms' competitiveness. The fragmentation of already existing monopoly positions has thus far been a virtual U.S. monopoly. Major structural breakups were ordered by the U.S. courts against Standard Oil (1911),[68] American Tobacco (1911), du Pont (1912), the Pullman Company (1944), the five leading motion picture producers (late 1940s), and American Telephone and Telegraph (1982), among others. Less comprehensive divestitures occurred in several other industries, and in more than one hundred cases, compulsory licensing of patents, sometimes on a royalty-free basis, was ordered.

Outside the United States, the only known divestiture under competition policy mandates (as distinguished from privatization and similar programs) was the forced spinoff of more than ten thousand British

---

66. Scherer and others (1975, pp. 117–18).

67. Scherer and others (1975, p. 112).

68. Although broken into thirty-four parts, Standard Oil of New Jersey was allowed to retain nearly all of its extensive overseas subsidiary network. In the most important early case *rejecting* divestiture, the U.S. Supreme Court was plainly influenced by mercantilist considerations: "And what of the foreign trade that has been developed and exists? . . . We do not see how the Steel Corporation can be such a beneficial instrumentality in the trade of the world, and its beneficence be preserved, and yet be such an evil instrumentality in the trade of the United States that it must be destroyed. . . . We do see [in dissolution] a risk of injury to the public interest, including a material disturbance of, and it may be serious detriment to, the foreign trade." *United States v. U.S. Steel Corporation et al.,* 251 U.S. 417, 453, 457 (1920).

public houses (pubs) owned by the six leading brewers.[69] Canada's competition policy enforcement office asked for special legislation to divest from the leading petroleum companies their interprovincial pipelines and half of their wholesale distribution facilities, but the effort was rebuffed by the Restrictive Trade Practices Commission.[70]

Merger Policy

For more than half a century the United States was also the only nation to have active merger control laws—first in the Sherman Act provision barring "combinations . . . in restraint of trade"; then in the 1914 Clayton Act's merger control provisions (rendered ineffective on technical grounds by Supreme Court interpretations in the 1920s); and most recently in the tough Celler-Kefauver Act of 1950, reinforced procedurally by the Hart-Scott-Rodino Premerger Notification Act of 1976. During the 1960s and 1970s, the number of formal challenges issued by the Department of Justice and Federal Trade Commission (jointly responsible for merger enforcement) averaged 20.7 a year.[71] Under judicial precedents shaped during the 1960s, horizontal mergers that combined substantial market shares came close to being ruled illegal, without regard to possible mitigating factors, unless one of the enterprises was on the brink of failing. In 1984, however, new Merger Guidelines issued by the Department of Justice added an efficiencies defense.[72] The defense has apparently been used only sparingly in administrative proceedings, and in the only known litigated test, a federal district court chose to make no decision on the contested efficiency issues.[73]

69. See "The Last Days of the Beerage," *The Economist*, May 20, 1989, pp. 69–70; and "Pubs and Brewers: They Told You So," *The Economist*, August 31, 1991, pp. 49–50. Jurisdiction over the relationship between brewers and pubs shifted later to EC competition policy authorities. See "British Pub Operators Protest Move for Brewers' Venture to Gain Exemption," *Antitrust and Trade Regulation Report*, October 7, 1993, pp. 477–78.

70. *The State of Competition in the Canadian Petroleum Industry* (1981, pp. 10–11); Restrictive Trade Practices Commission (1986).

71. Scherer and Ross (1990, p. 191). The challenge rate fell by roughly half in the early years of the Reagan administration.

72. U.S. Department of Justice (1984, p. 22), which states: "If the parties to the merger establish by clear and convincing evidence that a merger will achieve . . . efficiencies, the Department will consider those efficiencies in deciding whether to challenge the merger." It goes on to caution that "the Department will reject claims of efficiencies if equivalent or comparable savings can reasonably be achieved by the parties through other means."

73. *United States* v. *Archer-Daniels-Midland Company et al.*, 781 F. Supp. 1400 (S.D. Iowa 1991).

In other nations, merger controls came later and were characterized by schizophrenic implementation. In the United Kingdom, for example, beginning in 1964, the Industrial Reorganisation Corporation, and after 1975 the National Enterprise Board, actively encouraged large-scale mergers. As Ken George explains:

> Behind this initiative was the view that British companies were frequently too small to compete effectively against overseas competitors together with the conviction that market forces could not be relied upon to rectify such structural weaknesses.[74]

Meanwhile, in 1965 the Monopolies and Mergers Commission was assigned formal responsibility for reviewing mergers combining market shares of 33 percent or more (later reduced to 25 percent) to determine whether the mergers "may be expected to operate against the public interest." Some of the early mergers allowed to go through—for example, between British Motor Holdings and Leyland, the two largest domestically owned auto manufacturers; and among three firms (including the most prominent price cutter) with a combined 35 percent share of the U.K. ball and roller bearing market—suggest that building national champions received greater weight than maintaining multiple locally owned competitors. However, studies of what happened following such mergers have raised doubts about whether the large-scale, government-brokered mergers of the 1960s and 1970s in fact enhanced industrial strength.[75] There are indications that during the past several years, the Monopolies and Mergers Commission has focused to an increasing degree on the competitive effects of mergers referred to it, avoiding forays into other industrial policy considerations.[76]

French attitudes toward necessary company scales and the role of mergers were characterized in an influential book by the journalist Jean-Jacques Servan-Schreiber:

> What should we do? In a nutshell: achieve a real economic union and build giant industrial units capable of carrying out a global economic strategy. . . .
>
> The first problem of an industrial policy for Europe consists in choosing 50 to 100 firms which, once they are large enough, would be the most likely to become world leaders of modern technology in their fields. At the moment we are simply letting European industry be gradually destroyed by the superior power of American corpora-

74. George (1990, p. 106). See also Caves (1980, pp. 148, 183).

75. See especially Meeks (1977); and Cowling and others (1980).

76. See "Merger Regulation in the United Kingdom" (1990, p. 16). Compare George (1990, pp. 133–35).

tions. Counterattack requires a strategy based on the systematic reinforcement of those firms best able to strike back. *Only a deliberate policy of reinforcing our strong points*—what demagogues condemn under the vague term of "monopolies"—*will allow us to escape relative underdevelopment.*[77]

Even though France adopted a merger control program as part of its competition policy in 1977, it was at first enforced only weakly for reasons explained by Frederic Jenny, rapporteur of the Competition Council:

> If the French government has progressively abandoned the aggressive pro-merger industrial policy it favored in the '60s, there is still a lingering feeling among public officials that large firms are better able to withstand international competition than smaller firms and that therefore, in general, one should not interfere with the attempts of French firms to increase their size through mergers.[78]

Among the handful of transactions opposed between 1977 and 1989, most involved foreign acquirers, prompting a claim that "merger control was in fact used by the Minister in charge of economic affairs to further protectionist aims rather than to further competition."[79] However, after additional changes in French competition policy laws, the pace of merger enforcement appears to have accelerated in 1990, and there were several challenges to mergers among domestic enterprises.

Under provisions remaining from the original 1947 Antimonopoly Law, as amended in 1949, sizable mergers had to be registered with the Japanese Fair Trade Commission, whose mandate was to ensure that a controlling position did not result. When the commission launched its first test case, challenging the merger of Yawata Steel and Fuji Iron to form Nippon Steel in 1969, other government agencies contested the commission's initiative. The merger was permitted to proceed with certain modest stipulations, and during the next decade the commission attempted no additional challenges.[80] It is unclear whether any outright prohibitions have occurred since then, although conditions (for example, guarantees of customer access) were attached to a considerable number of mergers.

West German competition law was amended in 1973 to prohibit mergers that might create or strengthen positions of market dominance

77. Servan-Schreiber (1968, pp. 157–58, 159).
78. Jenny (1990, p. 185).
79. Jenny (1990); and Jenny (1991, pp. 122–23).
80. "Japanese Fair Trade Commission Decision on the Yawata-Fuji Steel Merger" (1970).

unless the merging enterprises could show that "the merger will also lead to improvements in competitive conditions and that those improvements will outweigh the disadvantages of market dominance."[81] The law was enforced vigorously. Between 1974 and 1985 the German Federal Cartel Office issued judgments prohibiting 69 mergers, of which 26 were fully enforced, 15 were reversed by the higher courts, 5 were overturned by the Economics Ministry (which has independent review power), and 15 remained pending at the time the compilation was made.[82] During the same period, 113 mergers were voluntarily withdrawn by the merging parties following informal discussions with the Cartel Office.

The 1957 Treaty of Rome provided no explicit guidance on how mergers were to be reconciled with European Community competition policy. Two acquisitions by U.S. companies (Continental Can in 1971 and Philip Morris in 1982) were challenged, first as an abuse of dominant market positions under article 86 of the treaty, and, with Philip Morris, as a competition-restraining agreement. Following the Continental Can decision, there was sporadic debate for seventeen years over whether an explicit merger control regulation should be adopted. France enacted a national merger control law in 1977 in part to preempt the common market authorities and to persuade them that a Community-wide program was unnecessary.[83] Some German officials, pointing to their own strong national enforcement effort, advanced similar arguments. Nevertheless, agreement was reached in 1989 on a regulation, effective in September 1990, declaring as incompatible with the common market "[a] concentration which creates or strengthens a dominant position as a result of which the maintenance or development of effective competition would be significantly impeded."[84] The regulation goes on to enumerate various factors the Commission shall take into account in reviewing mergers, including "the development of technical and economic progress provided that it is to consumers' advantage and does not form an obstacle to competition." It is unclear what practical meaning the "technical and economic progress" caveat will have. An earlier draft of the regulation had stated that mergers could be authorized "on the ground that their contribution to improving production and distribution, to promoting technical or economic progress or to improving the competitive structure within the common market outweighs the damage to

81. See Mestmäcker (1980); and Baur (1980).

82. Scherer and Ross (1990, p. 196), citing Monopolkommission data.

83. Jenny (1991, p. 115).

84. European Community Council Regulation 4064/89, December 21, 1989, reprinted in "Text of EC's Merger Control Regulation," *Antitrust and Trade Regulation Report*, January 11, 1990, p. 61.

competition."[85] The rejected language appears to mandate a more explicit trade-off between merger benefits and anticompetitive effects than the "take into account" wording ultimately chosen. Nevertheless, critics have expressed fears that competitive considerations will regularly and perhaps unconsciously be subordinated to industrial policy goals.[86]

The European Community's emphasis on mergers creating or strengthening a "dominant position," which follows earlier West German precedents, poses similar ambiguities. In particular, is the strengthening of a dominant position undesirable because it lessens competition and hence works to the disadvantage of consumers, or because strong, dominant firms might secure advantages that allow them to drive out weaker rivals? In its first post-1990 decision prohibiting a merger, the EC Commission observed that a dominant civilian airliner manufacturer could simplify parts inventory control for airlines concentrating their purchases on its aircraft, offer attractive package deals, and engage in price wars that its rivals were reluctant or unable to match. Thus the Commission seemed more concerned about protecting *competitors* than *competition* from the ravages of a possibly more efficient dominant firm.[87]

It is hardly surprising that the first European case precedents are unclear and pursue questionable objectives. Early U.S. efforts to interpret the strong Celler-Kefauver merger control amendments of 1950 exhibited much intellectual muddle. In its first major pronouncement on the 1950 merger law, the U.S. Supreme Court ruled against a merger on grounds similar to those articulated in the airliner case by the Commission:

> Some of the results of large integrated or chain [shoe retailing] operations are beneficial to consumers. Their expansion is not rendered unlawful by the mere fact that small independent stores may be adversely affected. It is competition, not competitors, which the Act protects. But we cannot fail to recognize Congress' desire to promote competition through the protection of viable, small, locally owned businesses. Congress appreciated that higher costs and prices might

85. Jacquemin, Buigues, and Ilzkovitz (1989, p. 69).

86. Compare Jacquemin (1990, p. 549) (warning among other things that "instead of an explicit cost-benefit analysis, surreptitious compromises would be sought"); Schmidt (1991); Fox (1992, pp. 709–49); and "Getting Away with Merger," *The Economist,* June 12, 1993, p. 92. See also "Conferees Address Harmonization of U.S., EC Competition Regimes," *Antitrust and Trade Regulation Report,* October 14, 1993, p. 499, in which EC commissioner Karel van Miert is quoted as saying that the efficiency-enhancing goals of mergers would get greater consideration in view of the high unemployment levels prevailing in the common market.

87. See Fox (1992, pp. 735–38); and Jenny (1992, pp. 8–10), discussing the disapproved acquisition of de Havilland by a French-Italian aerospace joint venture. Canada, in whose jurisdiction de Havilland resided, complained to the EC for its failure to coordinate the merger vetting process with Canada as an interested party.

result from the maintenance of fragmented industries and markets. It resolved those competing considerations in favor of decentralization. We must give effect to that decision.[88]

In the ensuing three decades there has been considerable backtracking and clarification, but the objectives and content of U.S. merger policy remain disputed and susceptible to abrupt changes, among other things, with shifts in the Supreme Court's ideological mix. Little more can be expected of regulators trying their hand at the game for the first time in other nations. What seems clear, however, is that the game will be played by disparate rules in diverse jurisdictions.

Procedures also differ. Since 1969 the U.S. antitrust agencies have employed a pre-merger notification system (accorded statutory authorization in 1976) that sets deadlines for the filing of detailed information on product lines, market shares, and the like. The EC has a similar system requiring different and even more detailed data in the early notification stages.[89] Other nations impose their own special requirements. The consequence is that clearing the various administrative hurdles is a costly, uncertain, time-consuming venture for mergers between multinational corporations. Cooperation to alleviate the procedural complexity might yield transaction cost savings.

Controlling Abuses by Dominant Firms

Although nations other than the United States have chosen not to break up existing monopolistic consolidations, many attempt to regulate abuses perpetrated by sellers holding dominant market positions. Here too the legal traditions differ.

The U.K. Monopolies Commission, the German Federal Cartel Office, and the EC competition policy directorate all have in principle the authority to mandate a reduction of dominant enterprise prices believed to be excessive. Utilizing new statutory powers gained in 1973, the German Cartel Office tried during the 1970s to force reductions in the prices of gasoline, automobiles, vitamin B-12, and tranquilizers, among others. It succeeded temporarily on some fronts, but Hoffmann-LaRoche, maker of Valium and Librium, successfully fought its case to the German Supreme Court, and the international petroleum companies won dismissal at the appellate court level.[90] Discouraged by its experience and perhaps chastened by strong criticism, the Cartel Office apparently ceased trying to function as a price controller. An alternative rationalization rooted more in the logic of inter-

88. *Brown Shoe Co. v. United States*, 370 U.S. 294, 344 (1962).
89. American Bar Association (1991, pp. 167–68).
90. See Kaufer (1980); and Schmidt (1983).

national trade than in domestic policy was offered by the Cartel Office, which reported in 1989

a decline in the number of proceedings instituted against enterprises on the suspicion that there were abuses of market-dominating positions. This seems to be due to the fact that in many markets of the Federal Republic there are excess capacities and the German market is generally open to foreign products. The resulting competitive pressure on all enterprises as a rule leaves little room for abusive practices.[91]

Abuse control efforts by the European Community also encountered setbacks,[92] and priority appears to have been shifted to other mandates. To the extent that competition policy measures abroad do enforce price control measures, they reach their maximum point of departure from the approach taken in the United States. Since 1927 U.S. policy has recognized the wisdom of a key Supreme Court decision:

The reasonable price fixed today may through economic and business changes become the unreasonable price of tomorrow. . . . Agreements which create such potential power may well be held to be in themselves unreasonable or unlawful restraints, without the necessity of minute inquiry whether a particular price is reasonable or unreasonable as fixed and without placing on the government . . . the burden of ascertaining from day to day whether it has become unreasonable through the mere variation of economic conditions.[93]

Recognizing the near impossibility of constant surveillance, U.S. enforcement efforts are directed toward deterring specific competition-restricting

91. OECD (1989a, p. 123).
92. See Fox (1986, pp. 990–94).
93. *United States v. Trenton Potteries Co. et al.*, 273 U.S. 392, 397–398 (1927). Similar difficulties were recognized by Justice Bowen, writing for the British Court of Appeals in 1892 on whether a shipping cartel's freight rates were reasonable:

And what is to be the definition of a "fair freight"? It is said that it ought to be a normal rate of freight, such as is reasonably remunerative to the shipowner. But over what period of time is the average of this reasonable remunerativeness to be calculated? All commercial men with capital are acquainted with the ordinary experience of sowing one year a crop of apparently unfruitful prices, in order by driving competition away to reap a fuller harvest of profit in the future; and until the present argument at the bar it may be doubted whether shipowners or merchants were ever deemed to be bound by law to conform to some imaginary "normal" standard of freights or prices, or that Law Courts had a right to say to them in respect of their competitive tariffs, "Thus far shalt thou go and no further." To attempt to limit English competition in this way would probably be as hopeless an endeavour as the experiment of King Canute.

Mogul Steamship Co. v. McGregor, Gow, & Co. et al., 23 Q.B.D. 598, 615–16 (1889).

practices, or fragmenting the market structures from which the power to set high prices flows, not toward the prices themselves. In this respect U.S. policy avoids the dilemma predicted by Franz Boehm, a founder of Germany's Freiburg School: "It is easier to hold a greased pig by the tail than to control a firm for abuse of a dominant market position."[94]

The "dominant market position abuse" provisions of EC law have been also deployed to combat price discrimination, predatory pricing, refusals to deal, and the imposition of territorial restrictions upon distributors. These are best treated in subsequent sections.

Vertical Foreclosure, Dealer Restrictions, and Other Vertical Restraints

Among the practices with which competition policy must contend are so-called vertical restraints. These include refusals by one firm to buy from certain "upstream" suppliers or sell to certain "downstream" customers; foreclosure through vertical integration of market access to certain sellers or buyers; agreements that a firm (usually a wholesaler or retailer) will deal exclusively in the products of a particular supplier and not in those of the supplier's competitors; limits imposed by a supplier on the geographic scope or marketing practices of its dealers; and resale price maintenance, or the mandating by a supplier of the prices charged by retailers selling its products. The reasons for and consequences of such practices are extremely complex, and economists' evaluations of their desirability diverge by much more than the quantum customary in a profession not known for unanimity of viewpoints.[95] It should not be a surprise, therefore, that national laws differ widely both internally over time and across jurisdictions.

Refusals to Deal

Refusals by a market-dominating enterprise to sell its products to bona fide would-be purchasers have been condemned by the EC authorities in several cases when the refusal was found to limit competition.[96] In an early precedent-setting case, Commercial Solvents Corporation (CSC) was the dominant manufacturer of a raw material needed to make an antituberculosis drug. After a failed attempt to raise the price of the raw material, it integrated vertically downstream to produce the drug

94. Quoted in personal correspondence from Erich Kaufer, July 1978.
95. For an attempt to sort out the issues, see Scherer and Ross (1990, chaps. 14, 15).
96. For an analysis of the leading cases, see Fox (1986, pp. 994–1004).

itself, at the same time announcing that it would no longer sell the raw material to the Italian drug maker that was now its competitor. The EC Court of Justice found this to be an unacceptable abuse of a dominant position.[97]

U.S. antitrust law has been invoked to prohibit refusals to deal in a more limited array of cases, notably those in which the refuser controlled bottleneck facilities that were both essential and not easily duplicated, because, for instance, of scale economies or geographic anomalies. Examples include the refusal of a Minnesota electric power company to allow municipalities to "wheel" competitive power over its high-voltage transmission lines, and barriers erected by integrated petroleum companies to the use of their pipelines by independent oil producers and refiners. The difficulty with such cases, like the CSC case, is that competitors can be barred from using the essential facility or purchasing the essential input by setting prohibitively high prices as well as by a flat refusal to deal. Thus competition policy enforcers are again thrust into the position of determining whether prices are "reasonable." The U.S. government, for example, struggled for more than half a century with the oil companies over pipeline access. Each government initiative (including having the Interstate Commerce Commission regulate pipeline access and rates) was met by strategic reactions from the petroleum companies that preserved at least some integrated company advantage over independents.[98] Some have argued as a consequence that, whenever possible, such essential facilities be structurally separated from the control of vertically integrated enterprises competing with other would-be users.

Refusals to deal are especially problematic when they are carried out by nationalized enterprises accorded a monopoly position by statute or government fiat. National monopolies may refuse to purchase or distribute importers' goods not only to favor their own upstream production facilities, if they exist, but also to implement chauvinistic "buy-at-home" policies when foreign firms compete with domestic enterprises. Eliminating such trade-distorting preferences has been a major priority of EC competition policy under its Single Market initiative.

Market-Foreclosing Vertical Mergers

Early interpretations of the U.S. Celler-Kefauver Act were as hard on vertical mergers that closed off market opportunities to remaining competitors as they were on horizontal acquisitions. Thus, in analyzing the

---

97. *Istituto Chemioterapico Italiano SpA and Commercial Solvents Corporation* v. *Commission of the European Communities,* 1974 E.C.R. 223.

98. See, for example, Mitchell (1979).

acquisition of Kinney, which owned more than 400 retail shoe stores, by Brown Shoe Company, the fourth-largest U.S. shoe manufacturer, the Supreme Court said:

> It is apparent both from the past behavior of Brown and from the testimony of Brown's President, that Brown would use its ownership of Kinney to force Brown shoes into Kinney stores. . . . Moreover, the [district] court found a tendency of the acquiring manufacturers to become increasingly important sources of supply for their acquired outlets. The necessary corollary of these trends is the foreclosure of independent manufacturers from markets otherwise open them.[99]

Thus six black-shoed justices (with two abstaining) voted to undo Brown Shoe's acquisition.

This and numerous other vertical merger prohibitions precipitated considerable critical comment from economists and legal scholars. As the literature evolved, it has become accepted that vertical mergers can have both good and bad effects.[100] On the positive side is the possibility of making marginal cost, rather than the higher price charged by an upstream monopoly, the criterion for use of an input. Thus the output-restricting double marginalization of upstream and downstream demands can be avoided, and choices of the proportions in which complementary inputs are mixed may be subject to less distortion. On the negative side, vertical mergers can under certain circumstances increase an upstream monopoly's power over unique "upstream" inputs not directly controlled, along with those that are acquired. For example, if aluminum and magnesium can be blended in varying proportions to make light fabricated metal products, acquisition of a controlling interest in product manufacturers might allow an aluminum monopolist to control the demand for magnesium (especially if magnesium has few other uses), and hence to extract rents from the magnesium producing stage.

Furthermore, in oligopoly situations, vertical integration redistributes the downstream entity's purchasing preferences toward integrated supply sources and away from nonintegrated competitors. Even when no misallocation of resources follows, this may be considered unfair. Thus if upstream prices uniformly exceed marginal cost (for example, because of scale economies, high R&D costs, product differentiation, or collusion), the unintegrated supplier's bid is evaluated on the basis of price, against which the multistage profit maximizer will compare its lower marginal cost from internal supply. Also, in vertically integrated enterprises that decentralize decisionmaking by using arm's length transfer prices, the

---

99. *Brown Shoe Co.* v. *United States,* 370 U.S. 294, 332 (1962).
100. See Scherer and Ross (1990, chap. 14).

integrated supplier has a second-mover advantage. If a nonintegrated firm cuts its price, even to marginal cost, to win an order, the integrated upstream firm can be put on notice and adjust its own price to a winning level. Upstream firms may therefore attempt to acquire their own captive outlets to defend themselves, precipitating a bandwagon effect that dries up the pool of available independent downstream enterprises. If the scale required to operate both upstream and downstream is large, barriers to new entry may rise. Recognizing these complex circumstances, the Department of Justice announced in its 1982 Merger Guidelines that it would oppose vertical mergers mainly when (1) vertical integration was so extensive that simultaneous two-stage entry was necessary; (2) two-stage entry was significantly more difficult than single-stage entry; and (3) the structure and other characteristics of at least one market were otherwise so conducive to noncompetitive performance that the increased difficulty of entry was likely to affect performance.[101] Few challenges have followed since then.

A quite different approach has been taken to vertical mergers in precedent-setting cases outside the United States. For instance, when British Motors Corporation sought in 1965 to acquire Pressed Steel Company, the largest British body stampings specialist, the Monopolies Commission let the merger go through when British Motors gave its assurance that other auto manufacturers would continue to be served by Pressed Steel on a nondiscriminatory basis.[102] Similarly, Japan's Fair Trade Commission acquiesced in the merger of Fuji and Yawata when the merged Nippon Steel Corporation agreed to supply rival steelmakers with pig iron and rails until they established their own facilities, and to provide know-how to a competitor entering the sheet pile business.[103] In both cases, the authorities tendered their approval on the basis of *assurances* from the merging firms that they would conduct themselves properly. U.S. policy has been more skeptical about whether assurances would be carried out, and hence more insistent that competition-threatening structural changes be precluded.

Vertical ties have been singled out as one reason foreign manufacturers have had difficulty importing into the Japanese market.[104] The distribution of consumer goods in Japan takes place predominantly through small retail outlets, which rely heavily upon wholesalers to provide merchandise on short notice. Japanese manufacturers frequently hold partial

---

101. U.S. Department of Justice (1982, p. 22).

102. U.K. Monopolies Commission (1966).

103. "Japanese Fair Trade Commission Decision on the Yawata-Fuji Steel Merger" (1970).

104. See, for example, OECD (1984, pp. 43–48); Matsushita (1986); and Lawrence (1991).

equity ownership positions in the wholesalers that carry their products. They also lend executive talent to the wholesalers.[105] At the manufacturing level, makers of complex products such as automobiles and video recorders often maintain minority stock positions in companies that supply component parts. Although integrated vertical profit maximization, considering marginal costs rather than quoted prices, seems unlikely when stockholdings are only partial, the relationships may confer upon quasi-integrated suppliers asymmetric advantages similar to those discussed two paragraphs previously. If so, an American-style remedy (to be sure, invoked at home only in compelling cases, and possibly ineffective in changing the more subtle relationships among Japanese firms) would be to require spinoff of the intercorporate stockholdings.

Vertical Restrictions

The first major competition policy enforcement action taken by the European Community was against vertical restrictions imposed by the West German consumer electronics manufacturer Grundig.[106] Grundig established distributorships in various EC member nations and prohibited those distributors from shipping Grundig products into other EC nations. Apparently as a consequence of this policy, the prices of Grundig products in France were from 20 to 50 percent higher than they were in West Germany. The EC Commission and Court of Justice ruled this territorial restriction contrary to article 85 of the Treaty of Rome. Had distributors been allowed to ship to other member nations, the Commission reasoned, the "parallel imports" would compete down the prices in high-price nations. Preventing such arbitrage was inconsistent with the objective of creating a truly common market. Subsequent regulations were issued to provide block exemptions for, and even to encourage, exclusive dealership arrangements as long as one of the vertical partners was small (for example, with sales of less than 100 million ECU), but the Commission has insisted that parallel imports not be precluded. In 1992, concerned about the wide differences among EC nations in the prices of a given automobile model, the head of the Commission's competition policy directorate wrote the manufacturers, asking (1) that they do nothing to prevent their dealers from shipping across borders, and

105. Matsushita (1986, pp. 6–8). Not mentioned in the report, but possibly of importance, is the fact that many Japanese "company men" given a "golden handshake" at age fifty-five go into business as retailers and wholesalers of the products in whose manufacture they previously worked.

106. See George and Jacquemin (1990, pp. 223–26); and OECD (1984, pp. 57–59).

(2) that they regularly publish their price lists for each model in each EC nation.[107] The manufacturers resisted, and further steps seem likely. In 1992 the Commission proposed to combat the wide variation in pharmaceutical prices among EC member nations by attacking, among other things, manufacturers' informal restrictions on parallel imports from distributors in low-price nations to high-price nations.[108] Again, it is too early to judge the consequences.

U.S. antitrust law also limits the restrictions manufacturers can impose upon their distributors, but the Supreme Court has exhibited radical shifts in its collective mind, and government enforcement agencies have accorded actions against such restraints lower priority than have their European counterparts. In a 1967 decision, the Supreme Court condemned as per se violations of the Sherman Act territorial and other restrictions imposed by the Schwinn bicycle company upon its distributors.[109] However, a decade later it reversed itself, approving territorial restrictions imposed by the television set maker Sylvania upon its direct dealers in an effort to build market share. Arguing that such restrictions should be analyzed on a "rule of reason" basis, the Court observed that there had been no showing, either generally or in the specific case of Sylvania, that vertical restrictions have or are likely to have "a pernicious effect on competition." They would therefore not be discouraged unless they had demonstrable "anticompetitive effects."[110] Nevertheless, in the United States, as in Europe and Japan, territorial restrictions continue to be illegal if they are imposed *collectively* by distributors as a means of avoiding competition among themselves, rather than being implemented unilaterally by a manufacturer seeking the most effective marketing strategy.

Conceptually different from dealer territorial restrictions, but often accompanying them, are agreements that the dealer will carry only a particular manufacturer's products, or at least not carry the products of competing manufacturers. Such exclusive dealership arrangements lie in a gray area of antitrust permissibility in the United States, risking prohibition if the manufacturer has a large market share or if securing access to distributors is difficult for newly entering or small manufacturers. With the law hovering above their heads, the principal U.S. automobile manufacturers refrained from making exclusivity a formal condition of their dealer franchises. This greatly facilitated the entry of Japanese autos into

107. "Europe's Car Market: Carved Up," *The Economist,* October 31, 1992, p. 73. For a confirming analysis, see Bourdet (1988, esp. chap. 7).

108. Brittan (1992).

109. *United States* v. *Arnold, Schwinn & Co. et al.,* 388 U.S. 365 (1967).

110. *Continental T.V., Inc. et al.* v. *GTE Sylvania Inc.,* 433 U.S. 36, 58, 59 (1977).

the U.S. market, which in turn had profound international trade and competitive implications.[111]

The situation in Japan is less than symmetrical, erecting one of the obstacles importers have encountered in their quest for access to Japanese consumers.[112] Under prevailing Japanese legal interpretations, formal exclusive dealing contracts by either domestic or foreign manufacturers can be prohibited if competitors are excluded and a firm's monopolistic position is enhanced as a result.[113] However, manufacturer-dealer relationships are seldom spelled out in precise contractual language, and there are many reasons why retailers—and especially the typically small retailers with limited shelf space—might wish to maintain informally an exclusive arrangement with their suppliers. Thus a Japanese Fair Trade Commission study group, repeating the question pressed upon Japan's leaders by the United States and Europe, asked whether or not the distribution sector is collaborating in a willful effort to exclude imported goods from the market—a situation that, if true, would violate the Antimonopoly Law.[114] Its answer seems plausible:

> There is much in this overseas criticism that deserves serious consideration, but there is also much that goes beyond the realm of competition policy and public policy. . . . Distribution structure and business practices are not artificially designed . . . in any country. Instead, they evolve naturally over the long years of history, having a certain rationality in light of the prevailing constraints that govern social behavior, and there is thus a limit to how much policy actions can influence these cultural-heritage aspects.[115]

Nevertheless, the Japanese government cooperated with the United States during 1989–90 in "Structural Impediments Initiatives," agreeing among other things to enforce competition policy vigorously to reduce distributional barriers inhibiting the importation of foreign goods. And to clarify for Gaijin the intricacies of competition policy rules toward vertical and similar restrictions, the Fair Trade Commission published a ninety-three-page English-language interpretation.[116]

111. This is stressed by Matsushita (1986, p. 6): "The easy accessibility of the U.S. distribution structure has clearly been one factor working to the advantage of Japanese companies wishing to export to the United States."

112. See the well-balanced discussion in Matsushita (1986).

113. Fair Trade Commission (1973, p. 13).

114. Matsushita (1986, p. 14).

115. Matsushita (1986, p. 23).

116. Fair Trade Commission (1991).

Resale Price Maintenance

Because both attempt to provide retailers some insulation from price competition, and thereby to make the retailers more willing to sell a manufacturer's products enthusiastically, exclusive territorial restrictions and resale price maintenance (RPM) are conceptually similar.[117] In the United States, the laws governing RPM have had a checkered history. Briefly, there was a presumption of illegality until 1937, when Congress passed the Miller-Tydings Act, legalizing RPM on trademarked or branded commodities in interstate commerce and "in free and open competition with commodities of the same general class produced or distributed by others." The law's intent was largely to protect small retailers from rising competition by low-price supermarkets, chain stores, and the like. In effect, the law tried to preserve a retail distribution structure similar to what prevailed in Japan during the 1970s. Yet the tides of retailing innovation advanced relentlessly, and so by the mid-1970s RPM persisted in only a handful of consumer goods lines. The federal statutes legalizing RPM were repealed in 1975. During the 1980s, Reagan administration antitrust officials chose not to enforce the antitrust prohibitions against RPM and showed their hostility by filing *amicus curiae* briefs in private suits challenging alleged cases of resale price maintenance. However, in one of the new Clinton administration's first acts, the Reagan policy was abrogated.[118]

In Japan, resale price maintenance has been illegal since the early days of the Antimonopoly Act, but numerous exceptions were granted, and apparently the law was not enforced vigorously by the Fair Trade Commission, especially against informal price understandings between manufacturers and their dealers.[119] To the extent that price competition from supermarkets and chain stores was inhibited, the growth of such outlets, which because of their broad inventories were more apt to carry imported goods, was slowed.[120] Yet there were other factors retarding the

---

117. See Scherer and Ross (1990, chap. 15).

118. See "Text of Assistant Attorney General Anne K. Bingaman's Address to ABA's Antitrust Section," *Antitrust and Trade Regulation Report*, August 12, 1993, p. 250.

119. Thus when the Fair Trade Commission chose not to intervene, a retailer whose supplies were cut off for selling at discount took the unusual step of seeking judicial sanctions against the largest cosmetics manufacturer. See "Japanese Court Orders Reinstatement of Discounter Terminated by Cosmetics Maker," *Antitrust and Trade Regulation Report*, October 7, 1993, pp. 479–80; and David E. Sanger, "Discounting Finally Makes It to Japan," *New York Times*, October 11, 1993, p. D1. See also James Sterngold, "Japanese Beer Drinkers Get Something New: Discounts," *New York Times*, April 24, 1994, p. D7.

120. See "Cheaper Shopping in Japan," *The Economist*, January 28, 1989, p. 15.

emergence of large discount stores in Japan, as in Europe.[121] Modest incomes and hence low automobile ownership at first, and later formidably congested streets and highways, undoubtedly had a more potent influence than resale price maintenance. Retailing innovation was also discouraged in Japan by the tough enforcement of the 1969 City Planning Law, which made it difficult to open new suburban supermarkets.[122] Change is occurring, albeit gradually.[123] Meanwhile, most consumer goods in Japan continue to be sold by small stores that are relatively unlikely to stock imported products.

Price Discrimination

Both competition policy and international trade policy have provisions discouraging price discrimination—namely, selling to diverse customers, or customer classes, at different prices. But the substance differs radically across the two policy domains, and objectives come into particularly acute conflict.

When the European Community was formed, it was expected that eliminating barriers to trade within the common market would automatically minimize dumping problems between member nations because dumped goods would return to arbitrage prices in the market from which they were dumped.[124] Internal antidumping regulations were adopted for a transitional period, but they (unlike antidumping rules aimed at nonmember nations) were phased out beginning in January 1970 and replaced by competition policy rules concerning intramarket price discrimination.

The Community's competition law views price discrimination by a dominant enterprise as an abuse of power. United Brands, respondent in a leading case, sold green bananas to its distributors at prices that varied considerably among EC member nations, depending upon local demand conditions. Other United Brands practices prevented the reshipping of bananas from one nation to another, and hence the arbitraging of price differences. Upholding a $1.2 million fine but rejecting a Commission order of specified percentage price reductions in the high-price nations, the EC Court of Justice concluded that "a rigid partitioning of national markets was thus created at price levels which were artificially different,

121. On France, see the insightful analysis by Jenny (1990, pp. 153–56).

122. Matsushita (1986, pp. 4–5).

123. See "Japan Shops the Wal-Mart Way," *The Economist*, February 6, 1993, pp. 67–68.

124. Commission of the European Communities (1972, p. 90).

placing certain ripener-distributors at a competitive disadvantage, since, compared with what it should have been, competition had been distorted."[125] Despite some confusion in its economic analysis, the Court's main goal, as in earlier parallel import cases, appears to have been perfection of the common market, from which approximate equality of prices across member nations should follow.

Quite different objectives motivated the principal U.S. price discrimination statute, the Robinson-Patman Act of 1936. The law's impetus was a Federal Trade Commission report tracing the advance of chain stores at the expense of "Mom and Pop" retailers, at least in part because the chains were able to purchase their merchandise on discriminatorily favorable terms. The explicit intent of Congress, as recounted by the law's co-sponsor, Representative Wright Patman, was to "give the little business fellows a square deal."[126] The FTC tried hard, if not always self-critically, to enforce the Robinson-Patman Act in accord with congressional intent.[127] In an early interpretation, Morton Salt's 6.25 percent discount to large-volume table salt purchasers was condemned by the Supreme Court, which observed that "Congress was especially concerned with protecting small businesses which were unable to buy in [large] quantities" whether "the particular goods constituted a major or minor part of [their] stock."[128] However, this and other case precedents were vigorously criticized by legal scholars and economists. Economists contended that, especially in oligopolistic industries, unsystematic price discrimination was an important instrument for upsetting collusive price structures; that preventing discounts to high-volume purchasers could inhibit efficiency-enhancing innovations in retail distribution; and that the other efficiency effects of systematic price discrimination could be positive as well as negative.[129] Later Supreme Court interpretations of the complex law moved away from simple "injury to competitors, not competition" criteria and opened up numerous loopholes. Large retailers deftly exploited the loopholes to retain their discounts while avoiding prosecution. FTC enforcement of Robinson-Patman declined sharply from forty-three complaints a year on average in 1961–74 to less than one a year between 1975 and 1986.[130]

125. Cited in Fox (1986, pp. 1005–06).

126. "Robinson-Patman: Dodo or Golden Rule?" *Business Week,* November 12, 1966, p. 65.

127. A survey revealed that only 6.4 percent of the companies cited in FTC complaints between 1961 and 1974 had sales in excess of $100 million. Thus enforcement was disproportionately targeted toward the very small businesses Mr. Patman sought to protect. Scherer and Ross (1990, pp. 494–508).

128. *Federal Trade Commission v. Morton Salt Co.,* 334 U.S. 37, 49 (1948).

129. Scherer and Ross (1990, pp. 494–508).

130. Scherer and Ross (1990, p. 516).

Antidumping law, like Robinson-Patman, is oriented toward protecting competitors—that is, domestic producers materially injured by discriminatorily dumped imports—and not toward maintaining competitive market processes. But beyond this similarity in intent, major differences intrude. The Robinson-Patman Act prohibits price discrimination "where the effect . . . may be substantially to lessen competition or tend to create a monopoly in any line of commerce." The national antidumping laws that have evolved from the various GATT agreements express no concern for preventing monopoly. More important, despite its protective intent, the Robinson-Patman Act allows a seller to rebut prima facie evidence of price discrimination by showing that its lower price "was made in good faith to meet an equally low price of a competitor, or the services or facilities furnished by a competitor."[131] A series of Supreme Court decisions has made this a powerful defense. Except for some special rules governing steel pricing within the European Community,[132] there is no provision in dumping law to exonerate discrimination that merely adapts to competitive situations. Thus, even with the originally protectionist Robinson-Patman law, latitude has emerged for the play of traditional competition policy goals. In virtually every major nation and the Community, which has brought roughly the same number of antidumping actions as the United States,[133] dumping law remains unambiguously protectionist.

There are other significant differences. To prevail in a Robinson-Patman Act complaint, one must prove discrimination. Even under the long-accepted meaning of discrimination—namely, lower net prices in the export market than in the home market—the evidentiary standards for proving dumping price differences, at least in the United States, are much weaker than those required in competition policy cases.[134] Although an attempt was made in the Uruguay Round negotiations to require fairness in the determination of dumping margins, the final 1993 text was compromised to let national tribunals retain considerable discretion.[135]

131. Public Law 692, 74 Cong., sec. 2(b). Under a 1983 Supreme Court interpretation of U.S. price discrimination law, firms may "meet" but not "beat" the price of a competitor. See Scherer and Ross (1990, p. 515). Under GATT, evidence of "significant price undercutting" can be proffered to show injury. GATT Secretariat (1993, MTN/FA II-AIA-8, p. 4).

In France, as in the United States, the early price discrimination law was used to protect small merchants. A 1985 amendment making discrimination illegal only if it was likely to "impair competition" was opposed by small distributors. Jenny (1990, p. 161).

132. See Stegemann (1968).

133. See Schmidt and Richard (1992, p. 223); and Messerlin (1989b, pp. 564–66).

134. See Murray (1991).

135. Compare Institute for International Legal Information (1992, pp. F.1–5); and GATT Secretariat (1993).

Anticipating the difficulties of comparing transactions across national markets, the Havana Charter (article 34, sec. 1[b]) and the original GATT treaty provided an alternative standard:

> The margin of dumping shall be understood to mean the amount by which the price of the product exported from one country to another . . . is less than . . . the cost of the product in the country of origin plus a reasonable addition for selling cost and profit.[136]

This "constructed value" standard was applied extensively during the late 1970s and 1980s after multinational negotiations established procedures for its implementation. It was retained with only modest changes in the Uruguay Round agreement of 1993. In normal U.S. practice, the constructed value of a product is derived by adding to operating expenses (including allocated production and selling costs) per unit a fixed general, selling, and administrative (GS&A) allocation of either 10 percent or prorated actual GS&A, whichever is higher, plus a profit margin of 8 percent on unit operating plus allocated costs.[137] This poses at least two substantive problems.

First, during the early stages of a new product's life cycle, producers tend to ride down "learning curves," with average full costs well above marginal costs. Once production experience has accumulated, full cost per comparable function may be appreciably less than the cost of earlier-generation products, but to gain acceptance in the market during the early learning curve stages, the new product may have to be priced below current full cost. When full-cost constructed value is taken as the standard for dumping,[138] it discourages the aggressive marketing of new products—a plainly anticompetitive and undesirable outcome.

136. "General Agreement on Tariffs and Trade" [1947, article 6, sec. 1 (b) (ii)].

137. Murray (1991, pp. 46–49). The final Uruguay Round draft agreement provided that the amount for administrative and selling costs "shall be based on actual data" and "the amount for profit . . . shall not exceed the profit normally realized by other exporters or producers . . . of the same general category in the domestic market of the country of origin." GATT Secretariat (1993, MTN/FA II-AIA-8, p. 2).

There is controversy over whether the arbitrary GS&A and profit minima used in past U.S. dumping determinations were realistic. The best source of evidence on U.S. manufacturing industry conditions is Federal Trade Commission (1985). In prosperous 1977, the last year for which data are available, 86 of the 238 industries surveyed had operating profits less than 8 percent of fully allocated operating costs. They would have to bear a higher profit margin than they actually earned under the constructed value standard. If one equates Line of Business "nontraceable" GS&A costs with *unallocated* GS&A costs, one finds that 98.7 percent of the industries had GS&A ratios less than the 10 percent constructed value standard. If one uses the more expansive definition including traceable plus nontraceable GS&A costs, one finds that 20 percent of the industries had GS&A ratios lower than the constructed value standard.

138. For example, in the semiconductor disputes of the mid-1980s. See Dick (1991).

The Uruguay Round final agreement provides that an "adjustment made for start-up operations shall reflect the costs at the end of the start-up period or, if that period extends

Second, overhead costs per unit are almost always higher when output is relatively low (during a recession) than in prosperous times, as any introductory economics student who has plotted a U-shaped short-run average total cost curve knows. Thus, under otherwise given conditions, constructed value is higher during a recession than during prosperity, which implies that prices should be higher in bad times—the opposite of what the law of competitive supply and demand dictates. In many normally functioning industries, prices do fall below fully allocated cost during recessions. Under the constructed value standard, this phenomenon is construed as dumping, even when sales are made at the same net price at home as in the export market. Consequently, one can have "dumping" without true discrimination, which led to U.S. charges during the recession of 1990–92 that Canadian steelmakers were dumping in the United States, and Canadian countercharges that U. S. steelmakers were dumping in Canada.[139] Although strange things happen under the Robinson-Patman law, nothing quite so strange has passed a Supreme Court validity test.

The usual remedy in a Robinson-Patman Act case is an order to cease discriminating, and in private suits the award of treble damages. The remedy in a dumping case is a tariff equal to the estimated dumping margin,[140] although many cases are settled by specifying trigger prices (in EC parlance, "price undertakings"), quotas, or other restrictions. Following an adverse Robinson-Patman Act judgment, there is nothing to constrain the respondent from competing as vigorously as it pleases, as long as it avoids discriminating. With tariffs, if the importer ceases discriminating, it continues to carry a competitive handicap relative to domestic firms and the status quo ante. Binding quotas and trigger prices also constrain the foreign seller's competitive exertions. Thus, although the price discrimination prohibitions under both competition law and dumping law inhibit the intensity of competition, the remedies applied in dumping cases tend to inhibit it more.[141]

Dumping is sometimes said to be "predatory," but the U.S. Antidumping Act of 1916 provides a more precise definition, namely, "com-

---

beyond the period of investigation, the most recent costs which can reasonably be taken into account." GATT Secretariat (1993, MTN/FA II-AIA-8, p. 2, n. 6). The latter criterion would perpetuate problems created by the Japan-U.S. semiconductor agreement of 1986, under which price floors were based upon costs in the previous quarter year, failing to reflect more recent learning-by-doing.

139. Clyde Farnsworth,"Canadian Steelmakers Aim to Dismantle Trade Barriers," *New York Times,* July 20, 1992, p. D3; Keith Bradsher, "U.S. Imposes Heavy Tariffs on Steel from 19 Countries," *New York Times,* January 28, 1993, p. A1; and "Canada Places Duties on Steel," *New York Times,* June 30, 1993, p. D2.

140. This is the U.S. practice. Criteria differ somewhat in other jurisdictions.

141. This point is emphasized by Schmidt and Richard (1992, pp. 223–29).

monly and systematically to import . . . articles . . . at a price substantially less than the actual market value . . . with the intent of destroying or injuring an industry in the United States."[142] Under prevailing U.S. law, predatory dumping is a criminal offense, and heavy burdens of proof must be met. As a result, the law was invoked infrequently. Until 1975 there had been no judicial interpretation.[143] Attempts to use the act against Japanese television exporters were unsuccessful—a controversy to which I return in a moment.

Much more experience exists with predatory discrimination claims under U.S. antitrust law.[144] In a 1967 Supreme Court decision, a relatively permissive standard, inferring predation from sales below cost (presumably, fully allocated cost) and intent to harm competitors, was applied.[145] Private actions alleging predation soared. Several were brought by computer peripherals manufacturers claiming injury from IBM's aggressive pricing behavior. The pending actions spawned a veritable industry of legal scholars and economists who wrote articles striving to formulate appropriate tests of predation. One school emphasized prices set below marginal (or average variable) cost; another pricing below average total cost combined with intent to monopolize; still others complex structural or strategic indicia. The trial and appellate courts did not agree among themselves, adopting at one time or another most of the rules suggested by scholars.[146] If any simple consensus can be inferred, it is that pricing below marginal cost (which among other things fails to maximize short-run profits) is almost surely predatory, while pricing below average cost but above marginal cost is either not predatory, or must be accompanied by other adverse indicia to be ruled predatory.

International trade policy collided with the predatory pricing debate in a case concerning the pricing of television sets exported by Japanese manufacturers to the United States.[147] The facts are complex and, despite protracted and sometimes chaotic litigation, poorly joined. It is clear that numerous Japanese companies formed, with more or less explicit encouragement from the Ministry of Trade and Industry, two cartels. One was

142. *Zenith Radio Corp.* v. *Matsushita Electric Industrial Co., et al.*, 402 F. Supp. 251, 254–55 (1975).

143. 402 F. Supp. 254. See also Victor (1983).

144. In the European Community, there were only two cases up to 1988. See Scherer and Ross (1990, p. 486); and Fox (1986, p. 1012). For a survey of cases in a dozen OECD national jurisdictions, see OECD (1989b, chap. 6).

145. *Utah Pie Co.* v. *Continental Baking Co. et al.*, 386 U.S. 685 (1967).

146. For a survey of U.S. decisions, see Hurwitz and Kovacic (1982). On proposed standards and rules applied in other nations, see OECD (1989b, chaps. 4–6).

147. *Matsushita Electric Industrial Co. Ltd. et al.* v. *Zenith Radio Corp. et al.*, 475 U.S. 574 (1986). See also Schwartzman (1992, pp. 54–57).

domestic. It almost surely elevated prices to monopolistic levels in the home market. The second cartel was in the export market, formed not to raise prices but to prevent the manufacturers from competing too vigorously among themselves for access to U.S. distributors and to avoid cutting prices so low that they would precipitate a dumping action. There was secret "chiseling" on the export cartel, however, so that prices did fall below the MITI-authorized "check" prices. U.S. television manufacturers were thrown into disarray by rapidly increasing imports from Japan. In 1975, as the Japanese share of U.S. color television set sales doubled in a single year to 36 percent, the operating income of the U.S. television and radio set manufacturing industry was 2.7 percent of assets. Only 28 industries out of 237 had a lower return.[148] Some domestic TV makers exited. Several redoubled their effort to stop the Japanese competition in the courtrooms.

Initial industry efforts to invoke the antidumping law had failed, in part because of procedural hurdles.[149] Partly for this reason and partly because they wanted to collect damages unavailable under the noncriminal dumping laws, the U.S. manufacturers sued under the antitrust laws, alleging predatory pricing. Hearing the case on appeal, a five-member Supreme Court majority embraced a simple theory to rebuff the plaintiffs. For predation to be rational (that is, profit maximizing), the Court said, the sacrifice of profits due to low costs during the predatory period must be compensated by the expectation of high profits once competitors have been suppressed or eliminated. The Court saw no evidence that after twenty years the Japanese firms had gained a position that allowed them to elevate prices and hence profits. Opining that "predatory pricing schemes are rarely tried, and even more rarely successful," the Court concluded that this one did not fit the success pattern, and therefore the Japanese producers cut prices "to compete for business rather than to implement an economically senseless conspiracy."[150]

A four-member minority seriously considered an alternative behavioral theory: that the cartelized high prices and reduced quantities sold at home freed up sufficient capacity to dump output profitably in the U.S. market. This plus the assumption that there were significant scale economies in television set production can be combined geometrically, in figure 4-4, to show that dumping in the U.S. market could be profitable indefinitely, that is, without the eventual price-raising demanded by the

148. Federal Trade Commission (1981, p. 32).

149. The procedural difficulties faced by television manufacturers were cited as grounds for making proof of dumping easier under new U.S. trade legislation passed in 1974.

150. 475 U.S. 589, 597–98. See also *Brooke Group Ltd.* v. *Brown & Williamson Tobacco Corp.*, 113 S. Ct. 2578 (June 1993).

Figure 4-4. *The Matsushita-Zenith Case?*

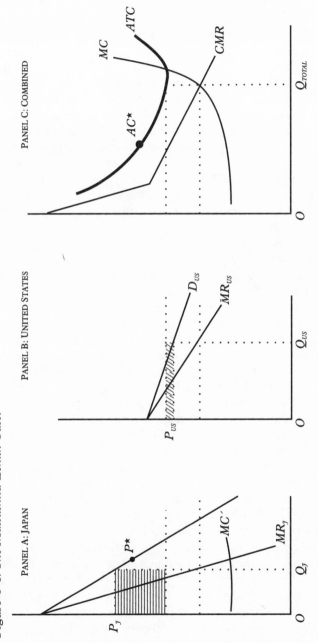

PANEL A: JAPAN

PANEL B: UNITED STATES

PANEL C: COMBINED

Supreme Court majority. Panel A represents the Japanese market, panel B the U.S. import market (with more elastic demand), and panel C the combined marginal revenue CMR, marginal cost MC, and average total cost ATC for the output in both markets. If the television makers sell only in Japan, the price will be P^* (panel A) and the average total cost AC^* (panel C). Given the large capacity, P^* is less than AC^* and an operating loss will be incurred. With price discrimination, the price will be raised to OP_J at home, and substantial sales will be made at the lower price OP_{US} in the United States. An accounting loss (diagonal shading, with price less than average total cost) is shown for the United States, but it is more than compensated by the lower unit costs attainable through greater capacity utilization and the higher price in the home market (horizontal shading). Thus the strategy is profitable in its own right, without any expectation of subsequent price increases in the U.S. market.

The available facts—for example, on how the prices charged in the United States related to marginal costs, on capacity utilization and economies of scale, and on the cost interrelationships between domestic and export production—are too sparse to know whether figure 4-4 portrays reality accurately. The most that can be said is that the majority's theoretical analysis is not the only plausible one.

If the long-run average total cost of television production and exporting from Japan is appreciably lower than the comparable U.S. cost after appropriate learning-by-doing has occurred and scale economy frontiers have been reached, the theory of comparative advantage implies that Japan *should* supply the U.S. market with television sets, and high-cost U.S. producers should cease production. Short-run marginal costs reveal very little about long-run comparative advantage. Yet a newcomer to some field, as Japan was in color television set production, may require time before it reaches minimum average cost and cultivates distribution channels. During this period, prices below average total cost do not necessarily signal a violation of comparative advantage. Determining whether pricing is sufficiently at odds with attaining market efficiency to be branded "predatory" requires a more broad-ranging inquiry into cost *functions* and market dynamics than a mere showing that prices were below some measure of cost. Because such inquiries demand sophisticated economic analysis, legal scholars have tended to shun them, preferring much simpler marginal or average variable cost tests instead.[151] Debate focuses on how much economic rationality to sacrifice for the sake of administrative feasibility. Since the stakes are high—no less than an efficient allocation of the world's resources—I favor investing resources to do the job right. I

---

151. See the exchange between Scherer (1976) and Areeda and Turner (1976).

would require those who allege sustained predation to support a rebutta-
ble presumption not only that (1) discrimination occurred and (2) that
the alleged predator's prices were below full-capacity average cost at the
extrapolated foot of its learning curve, but also that (3) the domestic
industry was at least as cost competitive as the foreign industry. For
allegations of predatory dumping over intervals too short to induce
significant structural change in the home industry, proof of prices
below average variable cost should be required.

Rule changes with a different logical basis could come through congressional action. A bill, S.2610, reported out of the Senate Judiciary
Committee in 1992 but not passed, would have amended the Antidumping Act of 1916, permitting private parties to obtain damages by
showing that imports sold in the United States for less than average total
cost "destroyed or injured commerce," and that the exporter's home
market lacked effective competition or was substantially closed to international competition.[152] An almost identical follow-on bill, S.99, was
introduced in 1993.[153] The average total cost test is more lenient than
those adopted by most federal courts in domestic actions claiming discriminatory predation. It would widen the gap between U.S. international trade law and antitrust law in the amount of protection against
price discrimination provided to *competitors*. How *competition* would be
affected will, one hopes, be debated vigorously.

Are Multinational Enterprises Special?

Following this review of the principal instruments of competition
policy, domestic and international, the question remains whether special
problems are posed by multinational enterprises (MNEs), that is, companies whose production operations transcend national boundaries.[154]

A plausible argument can be advanced that MNEs do intensify competition policy dilemmas. The intangible capital that makes it advanta-
geous for MNEs to extend their operations internationally may also
make them more likely to dominate the markets in which they operate.[155]
MNEs come into contact with their peers at numerous geographic

152. U.S. Senate (1992).

153. "International Fair Competition Act of 1993," S. 99, *Congressional Record*, January
21, 1993, p. S192.

154. The most prominent tensions engendered by MNEs come from their footloose-
ness—that is, their facility for shifting production to low-cost locations, perhaps causing
transitional unemployment at the locations forsaken—and their manipulation of transfer
prices on intra-branch international shipments to minimize national income tax burdens.
Neither issue is properly the concern of competition policy.

155. See Caves (1982, chap. 1).

locations, enriching the menu of possible strategic behavior interactions. For example, price incursions by company A in nation X might be countered by company B's retaliation in nation Y, where A is particularly vulnerable.[156] Among other things, operating in many markets increases the value of a reputation for reacting aggressively or even predatorily to competitive inroads in any single market.[157] The result may be more of a "live and let live" attitude than would exist when enterprises resident in single but diverse nations meet one another in the international trading arena. A concomitant may be the "spheres of influence" cartel arrangements common during the 1930s, in which national markets were staked off as a particular firm's domain and competitive international trade was suppressed.[158] And, as was observed in several EC competition policy cases, MNEs with strong positions in numerous markets are likely to exploit price elasticity differences among the markets through price discrimination, simultaneously taking steps to inhibit price-arbitraging parallel imports.

There is little hard evidence on whether these hypothesized behavioral proclivities are more prominent among multinational enterprises than among companies that have equivalent market positions but operate from only a single nation. It must be recognized that foreign direct investment by MNEs also brings competitive advantages, for example, by injecting new attitudes and vigor into national markets. In the belief that there is a special problem, the United Nations and the OECD have supported continuing studies of MNE structure and conduct. In 1986 the OECD issued a report proffering guidelines for MNE conduct on a number of dimensions, including competition policy.[159] The guidelines propose among other things that MNEs refrain from anticompetitive acquisitions and abuses of intellectual property rights, predatory behavior, unreasonable refusals to deal, discriminatory pricing, and preclusion of parallel imports. The guidelines are advisory and not legally enforceable. No cases are known in which national competition policy authorities chose to use them as a reference point in their enforcement efforts.

---

156. For theory and (equivocal) evidence from analogous cases of multimarket interactions within the United States, see Scott (1993, chaps. 2, 3); and Rhoades and Heggestad (1985).

157. On the theory, see Kreps and Wilson (1982); and Milgrom and Roberts (1982). Reciprocal entry deterrence does not appear to be typical of MNE behavior. To the contrary, there is evidence of herd behavior in entering new markets. See Knickerbocker (1973); and Baer (1984).

158. See Edwards (1955).

159. OECD (1986, p. 14).

Chapter 5

Policies for the Future

*T*HIS BOOK has identified numerous intersections at which conflicts appear among competition policy, nations' internal trade and investment strategies, and the collective desire of the world community to secure the benefits from free and open international trade.

With only occasional aberrations, competition policy works directly to keep markets open and maintain vigorous competitive interpenetration. Nations, however, frequently attempt to erect barriers to trade, protect national champions, and enhance the monopoly power of their domestic enterprises in export markets. The principal trade-distorting monopoly power problems reside in cartels linking enterprises of diverse nationality, especially those endorsed by one or more national governments; single-nation export and (less frequently) import cartels, especially, again, those with active support from home governments; informal understandings among multinational enterprises that divide up world markets into spheres of influence; similar restraints upon the international diffusion of technological know-how; and subtle vertical arrangements between domestic manufacturers and their distributors that make it more difficult for importers to secure access to consumer markets. There are serious substantive conflicts between the way antidumping laws are enforced and the parallel policies pursued toward price discrimination by competition policy authorities, both in national jurisdictions and in the European Community. Efforts by competition policy offices to prosecute foreign cartels whose effects flow through trade, or its impairment, to the competition authorities' home markets engender significant extraterritorial jurisdiction and international comity conflicts. A considerable amount of costly legal and bureaucratic duplication, including occasionally conflictingdecisions,[1] occurs when mergers must be vetted by the competition policy offices of multiple nations.

To keep these problems in perspective, one must recall Edward Mason's 1946 judgment that

> the injury inflicted by tariffs on domestic competition and American foreign trade has been several times greater than the effect of cartels; . . . current agricultural policy is likely to be [m]uch more damaging to exports than the total of American cartel practices; . . . intergovernmental commodity agreements will reduce the volume of postwar world trade more drastically than international cartels; and . . . the problem of dealing with state trading monopolies will far overshadow the difficulty of dealing with cartels.[2]

Mason's diagnosis was probably correct in its time. Since then, tariff barriers to trade have fallen dramatically, but so has the extent to which international trade is cartelized (with crude oil as a noteworthy exception, at least during the 1970s and 1980s). Distortions in agricultural trade have become even more serious with the escalation of export subsidy warfare, ameliorated only slightly by the cutbacks agreed upon through the Uruguay Round agreements. Trade barriers erected to protect state-owned enterprises continue to be problematic. One must not overestimate the payoffs attainable through competition policy reform.

The key question remains, what reforms are feasible? Is the community of trading nations ready to accept the kind of international organization contemplated under the Havana Charter? Had the charter been ratified, each member nation would have been obligated to ensure that the private and state-owned commercial enterprises within its jurisdiction did not engage in cartelization, the suppression of technology, and other restraints on international competition. An International Trade Organization would monitor compliance, and in the event of alleged violations, "request each Member concerned to take every possible remedial action" and "recommend . . . remedial measures to be carried out in accordance with [Members'] respective laws and procedures."[3]

Securing nations' consent to such an international organization will not be easy. The principal trading nations differ widely in their perceptions of the role free and open competition should play both domestically and in export endeavors. The substance of their competition policies diverges at least as much. And despite considerable success in the European Community's effort to implement common competition policies,

1. See Boner and Krueger (1991, p. 116).
2. Mason (1946, pp. 28–29).
3. U.S. Department of State (1948, p. 88).

the world's nations display continuing reluctance toward surrendering their sovereignty to an international enforcement agency. As Sir Leon Brittan, former head of the EC effort, observed:

> It is clearly not realistic to think in [EC competition policy] terms yet on an international scale. An international body with powers to seek out and destroy cartels may come one day, but the international community is clearly not ready to contemplate this possibility yet. For the time being, we should perhaps think about a clear agreement as to the rules relating to cartels, distinguishing between acceptable industrial cooperation and unacceptable restrictive practices along the lines already developed by all major systems of competition law. A simple rule agreed by all GATT members that restrictive practices and cartels thus defined are not enforceable at law would constitute considerable progress.[4]

Making cartels not enforceable at law would be a return to the weak approach pursued by Great Britain until passage of the 1956 Restrictive Trade Practices Act. A more ambitious yet limited step was recommended in 1991 by a special committee of the American Bar Association.[5] It would have all countries agree to repeal their statutes granting immunity to export cartels and to prosecute cartel conduct actively, both in the home market and for export. Seeing a world antitrust code as "the ultimate step in harmonization," the committee concluded that it is "quite unlikely that nations would come to agreement on meaningful precise antitrust standards beyond [the] narrow agreements proposed in [its] Report."[6] It cautioned that "it would not be wise to come to a bargaining table prepared to compromise, particularly when there is no compelling need to harmonize all antitrust law."

A Proposal

The skepticism expressed by Sir Leon and the ABA is well founded, and the ABA's recommendations can be seen as a plausible starting point for international negotiations. However, there is reason to believe that the world community has progressed sufficiently far in appreciating the

4. Brittan (1992, p. 10). For a slightly more optimistic view, see "Competition Policy Should Be International, Brittan Urges," *Antitrust and Trade Regulation Report*, November 25, 1993, pp. 692–93.

5. "Introduction and Recommendations of ABA Antitrust Law Section's Special Committee on International Antitrust," *Antitrust and Trade Regulation Report*, February 8, 1992, pp. 162–64.

6. "Introduction and Recommendations," p. 172.

benefits from vigorous competition to contemplate bolder steps. Securing an international agreement on competition policy rules has been identified by the Uruguay Round negotiators as a high-priority item for the post-Uruguay agenda. To move the ball forward toward the next round, I propose a set of international competition policies that recognizes individual nations' perceived need for exceptions and respects national sovereignty while moving as far as seems feasible toward eliminating avoidable restraints upon international competition.

PROPOSAL 1. Following ratification of an international compact, an International Competition Policy Office (ICPO) will be created within the ambit of the new World Trade Organization. It will have both investigative and (in a second stage) enforcement responsibilities.

PROPOSAL 2. One year after a new international competition policy agreement has been ratified, all substantial single-nation export and import cartels and all cartels operating across national boundaries must be registered, and the mechanisms of their operation must be documented, with the ICPO. "Substantial" means that any single enterprise, or confederation of enterprises participating together in a cartel, sustain international sales of $100 million a year or more in any relevant four-digit category of the Standard International Trade Classification. Furthermore, all substantial enterprises, or groups of enterprises subject to unified financial control, originating 40 percent or more of world exports in any four-digit SITC category, must register with the ICPO, providing details on their annual sales and the locations of their principal operations.

PROPOSAL 3. Following a petition by any signatory nation(s) that international trade has been restrained or distorted by monopolistic practices, the ICPO will undertake a study of the alleged practices, publishing the results of its investigation along with recommendations for correction. It will be assisted in the discovery of relevant evidence by the national competition policy agencies of signatory nations, or in the absence of such agencies, by other administrative and judicial authorities of the signatory nations.

Comment. Even though economists have disagreed about the costs and benefits of cartels and monopolistic practices and about the appropriate means for correcting monopolistic abuses, there was substantial agreement as early as a century ago that the first essential step toward dealing with the monopoly problem was the collection and publication of relevant information.[7] The Federal Trade Commission, for example, was originally proposed by President Woodrow Wilson as an information-gathering agency only. Antitrust responsibilities were added through a congressional compromise. In this recommendation, Wilson followed the maxim of Louis D. Brandeis:

7. See Scherer (1993, p. xiii); and Scherer (1990b).

> Sunlight is said to be the best of disinfectants;
> Electric light the most efficient policeman.[8]

Many national competition laws and the EC competition policy were implemented in the first instance by requiring the registration of cartel agreements or (for example, with the British Monopolies Commission) by making the details of their operation public, or both. Nations and industries adversely affected by registered cartel arrangements could through these ICPO functions learn of their existence and take appropriate defensive measures.[9]

PROPOSAL 4. Within three years after the creation of the ICPO, representatives of the signatory nations will agree upon a common format for reporting information on the supply and international trading activities of substantial enterprises that propose to merge. For all proposed mergers involving substantial enterprises thereafter, the designated information must be filed with the ICPO before the merger is consummated. The ICPO will in turn distribute the information to the competition policy offices of all affected nations.

PROPOSAL 5. Within five years after the creation of the ICPO, all signatory nations will enact national laws prohibiting export cartels operating from their home territory. Each signatory nation will be allowed three exceptions from this prohibition, each exception to entail activities not broader than a single four-digit SITC industry.

Comment. Nations will inevitably demand exceptions from the general anticartel rule. Because it would be virtually impossible to specify mutually acceptable criteria as to what kinds of industries should be exempted, this proposal leaves the choice of exempted activities to the individual nations but ensures that cartelization will not proliferate. Because the selected industries are likely to originate a higher share of total exports from less-developed nations than from industrialized nations, the rule is deliberately biased on income distribution grounds in favor of the less-developed nations.

PROPOSAL 6. Within five years of the creation of the ICPO, all signatory nations will enact laws prohibiting import cartels, except those created expressly to countervail the activities of export cartels *or* enterprises that alone, or in combination with other enterprises acting in parallel, dominate some segment of world trade.

Comment. This proposal assumes that the exercise of countervailing power can lead to improved world economic performance when substantial monopoly power persists, either within or outside the jurisdiction of

8. Brandeis (1914, p. 92).
9. See OECD (1984, p. 38); and Rabinowitz (1993, pp. 49, 63–65).

the ICPO, and that in such instances it is unlikely to cause impaired performance.[10] It assumes too that in tightly oligopolistic markets, monopoly power can be exercised through the "consciously parallel" behavior of enterprises with appreciable market shares.[11]

PROPOSAL 7. Beginning seven years after its creation, the ICPO will accept from signatory nations complaints about the alleged abuse of monopoly power by cartels or by any substantial enterprise originating more than 40 percent of world exports in a four-digit SITC category. The ICPO's enforcement division will investigate the complaint, obtaining the assistance of national enforcement and judicial authorities in securing relevant evidence. On the basis of its investigation, it will determine whether an abuse exists, and if so, recommend corrective measures. If national authorities fail to take appropriate corrective action, the World Trade Organization will authorize appropriate sanctions by injured nations against any nation(s) from which the abusive practices originate. Appeals from sanctions so mandated will be heard by the World Court.

Comment. Despite the considerable difficulty of determining when monopoly power has been abused, it is unlikely that widespread agreement could be secured for a flat "prohibition" standard. Sanctions reaching only the most egregious abuses probe the limits of national tolerance. The unqualified prohibition against all but three excepted export cartels per nation leaves the collection of policies proposed here stronger than it would be if all cartels were judged according to an abuse standard.

PROPOSAL 8. Beginning seven years after its creation, the ICPO will accept from signatory nation authorities complaints about notified substantial mergers whose probable impact will be to concentrate 40 percent or more of the world trade in some four-digit SITC category under the control of a single enterprise or group of jointly acting enterprises. If the ICPO determines that competition in international trade is likely to be jeopardized by such mergers to the detriment of consumers, it will recommend corrective measures to signatory nations, which will use their national laws and policies to remedy the problem.

Comment. Unless symmetry between cartel policy and merger policy is maintained, nations may react to anticartel enforcement rules by encouraging mergers. Merger waves followed an asymmetry of laws in the United States, Germany, England, and the European common market.[12]

PROPOSAL 9. Should a substantial enterprise continue to control 40 percent or more of world trade in some four-digit SITC category for a period of longer than twenty years on the basis of validly issued patents

10. See Scherer and Ross (1990, chap. 14).
11. Scherer and Ross (1990, chaps. 6–9).
12. Scherer and Ross (1990, pp. 155–61).

or copyrights, any signatory nation may require the compulsory licensing of the enterprise's patents or copyrights within its jurisdication at reasonable royalties.

Comment. It is improbable that nations would agree to the structural fragmentation of dominant enterprises residing within their borders. Continued dominance of a world market is likely to result only from superior performance, the control of unique natural resources, or the control of intellectual property. Superior performance is desirable and should not be challenged. Little or nothing can be done internationally about the control of unique natural resources. Patent and copyright protection for a considerable time is justified as an inducement to innovation. However, dominance can be perpetuated, with undesirable consequences for both pricing and the rate of technological progress,[13] through the accumulation of patents and copyrights on improved products and processes. This proposal will constrain monopoly power that persists beyond the intended life of original patent grants.

PROPOSAL 10. Beginning seven years after its creation, the ICPO will receive complaints from the competition policy authorities of signatory nations concerning monopolistic practices that distort international trade but that are not expressly covered by the policies specified here. It will investigate those complaints and make recommendations for appropriate corrective action by the competition policy authorities of nations in which the alleged practices occur. If the ICPO finds that international trade has in fact been distorted and if the problem is not remedied through national action, individual nations will be authorized to take appropriately graduated countermeasures against the nation(s) or industries in which the distorting practices occur.

Comment. This catchall provision is intended to cover the many complex practices upon which a general international consensus would be difficult or impossible to achieve. It limits signatory nations' ability to engage in aggressive unilateralism, for example, under Section 301 of the U.S. trade laws. It seeks to reduce the risk that unilateral action will evoke retaliation, mutual recrimination, and a breakdown of harmonious trading relationships.[14]

PROPOSAL 11. None of these proposals prevents any signatory nation from implementing more stringent rules with respect to restraints of competition within its national market. Nor do they prevent any signatory nation from adopting weaker rules with respect to restraints of competition whose effects occur solely within its national market.

13. Scherer and Ross (1990, pp. 630–60).
14. See Bhagwati and Patrick (1990).

Comment. International trade and investment delimit the domain of the proposed policies; infringement on national choices with no significant cross-border effects should be minimized. However, purely domestic cartels that lead to dumping overseas would be subject to international competition policy rules as well as to the standard remedies for dumping.

Other Policies

This set of proposals attempts to identify changes that would be acceptable to most important national participants in world trade and at the same time to solve the principal problems attributable to restraints on international competition. The implementation of its provisions is time phased, giving nations an opportunity to observe the process evolve before committing themselves to the full enforcement program, and reflecting the gradual pace at which both individual nations and the European Community have introduced and expanded their own new competition policies.

The proposals are not intended to be the last word on a complex subject. Rather, they are offered as a framework on the basis of which international competition policy negotiations can proceed.

For some of the proposed international measures, the unilateral exercise of extraterritorial jurisdiction against overseas cartels whose conduct injures U.S. consumers or producers is a plausible alternative. Even though certain nations (notably, the United Kingdom, Canada, France, and Australia) have erected defensive measures, such suits can be effective when major participants in foreign-based cartels have at risk significant investments in the United States and maintain U.S. branch offices sufficiently "in the loop" to allow for testimony and documents needed to prove Sherman Act violations to be subpoenaed. Bills such as S.99, pending in the 1993–94 Congress, would carry the exercise of extraterritorial jurisdiction further. They would permit private parties injured by dumping, augmented by other anticompetitive practices, to sue and recover damages from foreign firms. Unless the criteria defining "predation" are more stringent than the average total cost rules written into the draft bills, such measures would harm U.S. consumers and inhibit vigorous foreign competition in their attempt to protect U.S. business firms. It is preferable to limit the reach of extraterritorial litigation to cartels and other activities that plainly subvert the accepted goals of competition policy. It would be better still, in place of unilateral action, to foster an international accord under which governments waive sovereign immunity and act-of-state defenses in connection with challenges by other nations' subjects to alleged export cartel conduct.[15] And to prevent bills like S.99 from working mischief, international agreements on standards for actionable predation should be sought.

Along similar lines, action should be taken through future GATT framework negotiations to define more carefully the conditions under which "dumping" can be proved. Constructed value rules requiring full-cost pricing during recessions and in learning-by-doing situations (for example, in the early stages of technologically advanced product life cycles) should be eliminated as unnecessary and inappropriate inhibitions upon international competition and innovation.

The antisubsidy responsibilities assigned to competition policy authorities by the EC Commission have been consciously excluded from the international competition policy proposals made here. Combating trade-distorting subsidies, I believe, is better left for traditional countervailing duty mechanisms, at least until tariff and nontariff barriers to trade have been swept away, and unfettered world markets exist.

15. This is a recommendation of the ABA Antitrust Law Section's Special Committee. See "Introduction and Recommendations," p. 164.

Comments

Alexis Jacquemin

F. M. Scherer presents an excellent analysis of the main challenges confronting competition policy in a globalized world. He also offers a fruitful historical analysis of national and international trade and competition policies in the United States and Europe. In his final chapter, in response to the successful Uruguay Round and the high priority given to an international agreement on competition policy rules in the post-Uruguay agenda, Scherer makes a set of stimulating proposals that he considers acceptable to the most important national participants in world trade. I have no serious disagreement. In what follows, I first discuss the fact that competition law cannot be separated from other microeconomic policies and that the interaction among competition, commercial, and industrial policy creates substantial constraints for international agreements. In view of the European experience, I can be more explicit about the conditions for their compatibility. Second, I raise several issues about the policy options presented in the book, suggesting that some different views must be taken into account and that a more specific analysis could identify the advantages and limitations of alternative institutional designs in the domain of transnational competition policy.

Interaction among Competition, Industrial, and Trade Policy

Competition policy is probably the most impersonal and least discriminatory means of social regulation of an economy. As the pace of

Alexis Jacquemin is professor of economics (Louvain) and an adviser in the Forward Studies Unit of the Commission of the European Communities.

globalization quickens and transactions increasingly span national boundaries, competition policy becomes an obvious candidate for some form of international coordination.

Competition policy, however, interacts with other more interventionist microeconomic policies, mainly industrial policy and trade policy. That is especially true for such areas as state aid, public procurement, utilities, and antidumping, but also for cooperation in research and development (R&D) or the use of an efficiency defense in controlling mergers. Any effort to establish enforceable global competition rules must take into account these interdependences. Conversely, it would be dangerous to single out competition policy as a topic on its own without considering the great diversity in the interaction of national industrial and trade policies.

All public authorities must be concerned about the problem of coherence among their policies, be they micro- or macroeconomic. Contradictions between them lead to inefficiencies of each instrument, put into question their credibility, and create a climate of insecurity for the economic actors. Conversely, exploiting the possible complementarity among the various public policies can correct individual deficiencies, facilitate the enforcement of the policies, and increase institutional credibility.

A legal basis exists for the European Community's competence in the domains of competition policy (article 85 of the Treaty of Rome), trade policy (article 110 of the same treaty), and, since Maastricht, industrial policy (article 130 of the Maastricht Treaty). Given such an overall competence and the fact that the implementation of these different Community policies is centered in the EC Commission—an institutional situation quite different from that in the United States—one would expect the unavoidable tensions between policies to be controllable, so that a balance could emerge among the economic, social, and political concerns. But in practice the record is mixed.

As for the links between *competition policy* and *industrial policy*, clearly all industrialized countries, including Germany and the United States, have some forms of industrial (or structural) policy. They seek to encourage industrial developments through such devices as tax policies, R&D incentives, public procurement practices (especially in the defense area), credit policies, support of small and medium-size enterprises, and technical regulation and standards. But the degree of interventionism varies greatly from one country to another and over time. At one extreme is a situation in which competition among states is preferred to competition among firms: building large enterprises is encouraged through a lax merger policy, public procurement policy is used to build up or support national champions, and standards favor domestic over foreign suppliers. At the other extreme, competition policy plays the central role in maintaining an open, dynamic business environment. A strict control is exercised on subsidies, cartels, mergers, and other practices that could create market distortions. In the middle, there remains the question of efficiently correcting market failures arising from such problems as important externalities, nonconvexities in production and organization, and the consequences of uncertainty and asymmetric information.

It is fair to say that a consensus is growing among industrialized countries that market competition exerts a positive influence on social welfare and that targeted, interventionist industrial policies must be avoided. Nevertheless, considering directly or indirectly the different kinds of "market failures," all national legislations tolerate some behavior-restricting competition, even when the restriction is not minor. The corresponding criteria allow a large degree of discretion in interpreting antitrust rules. The more weight that is given to such an "efficiency" or "public interest" defense, the greater is the interaction between competition policy and industrial policy. Given the extreme diversity of policies intended to correct actual or perceived market failures, the probability of establishing minimum standards and enforcement for competition policy at the global level is severely reduced.

A European illustration is given by article 85 of the Treaty of Rome, which contains a broad prohibition of explicit and tacit collusion. In contrast to section 1 of the Sherman Antitrust Act, however, article 85 also contains an exemption from this prohibition for collusive behavior that generates sufficiently beneficial effects. An important application briefly mentioned by Scherer is cooperation in R&D, a principal vehicle for international competition.

An argument for permitting cooperative research is based on a problem of market failure associated with the appropriability of the benefits of R&D. The crux of the argument is that the amount of research performed by private firms and the diffusion of the knowledge generated by them may be socially inefficient over a broad range of market structures, including competition. The reason is simple. On the one hand, a firm will conduct R&D only if it can appropriate enough of the benefits; such appropriation requires a limited diffusion of R&D output. On the other hand, nearly perfect appropriability impedes socially costless spillovers of R&D results to other firms. Cooperative R&D can then be viewed as a way to internalize the externalities created by significant R&D spillovers while providing a more efficient sharing of information among firms.

Michael L. Katz, and Claude d'Aspremont and Alexis Jacquemin, have established conditions under which a cooperative agreement could raise social welfare through its effects on the equilibrium level of R&D.[1] In the presence of sufficient positive spillovers of R&D benefits, firms cooperating in R&D but not in output spend more on R&D than non-cooperative firms do; they also produce more output, thus arriving closer to the socially optimal level. As for the collecting and sharing of information in research consortia, Xavier Vives suggests, using a simple model, that information pooling creates competitive advantages and that active promotion by government of information collection and dissemination can be socially valuable.[2]

Although cooperative R&D has potential advantages from society's standpoint, it can also lead to a socially harmful reduction of competition, especially if it means an extended collusion between competitors in creating common policies at the market level. In this domain, national regulations differ widely. European Regulation 418/85, which must be respected by all firms in the European Economic Area (EEA), provides a compromise between cooperation and competition in research.[3] It exempts not only joint R&D but also joint exploitation of the results of that R&D.[4] Underpinning the regulation is the belief that cooperation in R&D should not always be limited to R&D, narrowly defined; joint exploitation of the results may be needed to stabilize an agreement and to solve the appropriability problem. In the case of such R&D cooperation with corporations of third countries, regulatory inconsistencies can then create uncertainties that could deter and destabilize those agreements.

A contrasting illustration relates to the control of mergers. Clearly some efficiency gains can be expected from a merger. But when a firm creates a dominant position, the European regulation does not provide a derogation from the prohibition on the basis of efficiency effects. Imagine a transcontinental merger in which a Canadian firm is involved and is creating a dominant position: the lax Canadian antitrust policy could permit the operation in the name of efficiency and industrial policy considerations, whereas the EC authorities could block it.

In that context European industrial policy may be briefly examined. Article 130 of the Maastricht Treaty states that the conditions needed to make EC industry competitive are met in a system of open and competitive markets. It also says that this new title "shall not provide a basis for

1. Katz (1986); d'Aspremont and Jacquemin (1988).

2. Vives (1984).

3. Commission Regulation (EC) 418/85 of December 19, 1984, *Official Journal*, L 53/5, February 22, 1985.

4. Article 1(2)(d) of Commission Regulation 418/85 specifies that "exploitation of the results" means the manufacture of the joint venture product or the licensing of intellectual property rights to third parties. According to Regulation 151/93, the exemption is standard, under conditions, so as to cover joint distribution of products resulting from joint research.

the introduction by the Community of any measure which could lead to a distortion of competition."

Such an approach, insofar as it is respected, could overcome the view that the intellectual godfather of industrial policy is strategic trade theory. In its 1990 communication to the Council of Ministers on "Industrial Policy in an Open and Competitive Environment," the EC Commission states that the main responsibility for industrial competitiveness must lie with firms themselves, but that they should be able to expect from public authorities clear and predictable conditions for their activities. The conditions include the establishment of trans-European networks, the promotion of cooperation in R&D, and the introduction of large-scale educational and training programs. These actions are intended to have a horizontal diffusion effect on the whole industry, including services. A priori, there is no reason why EC industrial policy should harden EC trade policy. On the contrary, it is compatible with a continuous effort to further open up and strictly implement the multilateral trading system. However, the future attitude will probably depend on the policies adopted by the two other members of the triad—North America and Asia— and the implementation of the GATT (General Agreement on Tariffs and Trade) decisions.

This leads to the relationships between *trade policy* and *competition policy*. Compared with rule-based competition policy, trade policy, like industrial policy, normally allows more discretionary power. According to article 113 of the Treaty of Rome, "the common commercial policy shall be based on uniform principles," but the trade rules do not exclude the adoption by the Council of Ministers of anticompetitive protectionist measures. In fact, maintaining intra-EC competition is a much more accepted goal than safeguarding competition from outside.

The pressures for not disrupting economic transactions between EC member states could lead to a difficult choice between the erosion of intra-EC free trade and the erosion of free trade with the rest of the world. One unfortunate implication is that, in several domains, not only do trade and competition policy follow different roads, but they can also interact in a perverse way. Although a free trade policy is part of competition policy, the use of instruments such as antidumping duties and voluntary export restraints not only affects extra-EC trade but, through a feedback effect, could mitigate competition within the Community.

Some authors (for example, Patrick Messerlin) argue that European antidumping (allowed by article 6 of GATT) actions have a pro-cartel and promerger propensity.[5] Such actions increase the cartelization capac-

5. Messerlin (1989).

ity of firms unable to collude without some kind of public support; they also could induce EC firms to merge with foreign firms operating in EC markets to the extent that EC-owned foreign exporters are more immune to antidumping measures. Furthermore, as argued by Richard Caves, using trade policy for solving specific problems is less efficient than making industrial policy corrections, "a conclusion of many years' discussions that plays to the new-found interest in policies focused directly upon distortions in the domestic market of open economies."[6] In many circumstances, such as external economies or diseconomies, the specific market failure is indeed associated with insufficient domestic output rather than with excessive imports. Domestic tax and subsidy correctives are then usually preferable to international trade restrictions. A classic example is a situation in which the industry's output is indeed suboptimal;[7] then the use of, say, a tariff to enlarge domestic production is a second-best remedy, because it creates an undesirable contraction in domestic consumption at the same time as it accomplishes its stated goal of expanding domestic production. A domestic production subsidy in this instance is the first-best solution.

Conversely, competition policy can be used for market access and can then reduce the temptation to maintain an aggressive trade policy. The insertion of competition clauses in the agreement on the EEA, for example, allows the Community not to apply its antidumping and antisubsidy legislation to imports from the EFTA (European Free Trade Area) countries of products originating in one of those countries. This decision implies opting for competition rules and harmonized legislation rather than commercial policy tools to regulate trade within the EEA. In the free trade area they established, Canada and the United States did not agree on common competition rules, so that their respective antidumping and antisubsidy legislations continue to apply in trade between them.[8]

A geographic extension of a common competition policy to a growing number of countries also permits eliminating negative external effects created by an absence of competition rules or by an ineffective enforcement of rules. A well-known example is the export cartel. According to articles 85 and 86 of the Treaty of Rome, the EC competition policy ensures only that competition within the common market is not distorted (see article 3[F] of the treaty). It does not require that EC companies act in a certain way abroad, unless their actions affect trade between member states. Under the Webb-Pomerene Act, the Export Trading Company

6. Caves (1987, p. 7).
7. Johnson (1965).
8. Bourgeois (1993).

Act, and the Foreign Trade Antitrust Improvement Act, foreign plaintiffs injured by U.S. conduct that has no U.S. effects have no right to recover under U.S. antitrust laws. The example of a pure export cartel given by Scherer could be enlarged by including the more common case of a mixed cartel; that is, when domestic demand accounts for a proportion of world demand. It is still in the interests of national authorities to accept the mixed cartel if domestic sales represent a relatively minor proportion of foreign sales, such that the surplus gained by domestic producers on foreign markets is higher than the surplus lost by domestic consumers. But once a common competition policy is adopted between the concerned countries, such situations are "internalized." If this first-best solution is not feasible, one possibility is to initiate GATT proceedings. In 1983 the EC requested the establishment of a panel, arguing that Japan's failure to prevent anticompetitive practices in its internal market impeded EC products to enter the Japanese market. In the end, the EC refrained from pursuing the case. As will be seen, doubts exist about using GATT to address competition policy–related concerns, one problem being that purely private business practices that are not supported by the government cannot be challenged.

At this point a preliminary conclusion can be drawn: attempts to internationalize competition laws and their applications will affect other crucial domains of public policies, and for such laws to have a chance of success the most important potential interactions and trade-offs must be made explicit.

Policy Issues

According to data collected by the U.S. Federal Trade Commission (FTC) in 1991, of the 1,500 transactions filed under the Hart-Scott-Rodino Act of 1988 with United States antitrust agencies, 340 included foreign elements, of which 160 involved firms located in the EC.[9] And, as shown by many recent cases, the potential for conflict of jurisdiction increases as national competitive laws acquire broader geographic jurisdiction. For example, Siemens and General Electric Company referred their bid for Plessey separately to the British, German, French, and Italian, as well as to the EC Commission, competition authorities. Any authority acting in isolation can terminate the merger, including individual U.S. states, which, following a Supreme Court decision in 1990, now have the ability to disband a merger. In 1989 a private antitrust case launched in New York State successfully prevented a merger, not chal-

9. See Steiger, chairman of the Federal Trade Commission, quoted by Rill (1993).

lenged by the U.S., British, or Commission authorities—the Minorca SC acquisition of Consolidated Gold Fields. In another case, on August 31, 1990, the FTC required Institute Merieux SA, which had purchased Connaught Labs (neither company had production facilities in the United States), to lease a rabies vaccine business in Toronto to a third party and to give jurisdiction to the FTC for ten years over any future mergers of the company. Institute Merieux and Connaught Labs had the dominant share of rabies vaccine in the United States. However, this extraterritoriality did not entail coordination with Canadian authorities. The Canadian competition authorities did not see a competition problem, even though the firms had the same dominant market share in Canada as in the United States. In addition, the U.S. remedy might have killed the deal, which was welfare enhancing for Canada and France.[10]

Other examples can be given, like the Gillette-Wilkinson (1990–92) or the Renault-Volvo (1990) cases. A recent one is in the area of reinsurance. The case involved complaints filed by nineteen U.S. states alleging that the defendants—U.S. primary insurers and a reinsurance broker, and Lloyd's of London reinsurers—had violated the Sherman Antitrust Act. They were accused of a conspiracy. Unfortunately, the Supreme Court failed to provide the fundamental statement of the law on the extraterritorial application of U.S. antitrust laws that businesses and governments on both sides of the Atlantic had been hoping for. It confined its decision to the particular facts of the case.

An economic analysis of some of these cases could be useful in determining the expected benefits from an international competition policy. A priori, three types of benefits can be identified.[11] First, the private transaction costs of compliance could be lower because of a higher level of transparency, a reduction of learning costs, a lighter procedural burden, and less uncertainty. Second, common rules, coordinated surveillance, and enforcement could also reduce the costs of undesirable regulatory arbitrage: evasion, externalization, and extraterritoriality. Third, a cost reduction of several compliances that result from overlapping and differing regulations could be obtained.

But to appreciate the proposals made by Scherer and the prudence of a phase-in time intended to let nations observe the process evolve before making a full commitment, it is useful to say a word about alternative approaches.

One approach suggests that further moves to liberalize trade and to implement existing GATT disciplines may have a much greater effect on global competition than will the pursuit of multilateral competition

10. Waverman (1993).
11. Trachtman (1993).

policy disciplines. It is the old idea that the best antitrust policy is free trade and free market access. But even with free trade, international competition will be affected by market imperfections and market failures that create static and dynamic inefficiencies. The exogenous characteristics of demand and supply, as well as the strategic moves allowed by these characteristics, lead to international concentration, barriers to entry and exit, product differentiation, and asymmetric information. Therefore, there is no guarantee that free trade and free market access will, by themselves, lead to a social optimum.

Two GATT instruments could be used to obtain market access. The first is to charge the contracting party with having violated a GATT obligation. It is the approach suggested by Joel P. Trachtman. He argues that exemptions or nonenforcement of competition policy could theoretically constitute a de facto subsidy to a domestic industry. On this basis, exemptions could be the subject of nullification and impairment or other claims and could be countervailed once they are identified. But Trachtman adds that, even if some of these "subsidies" can be included in the definition of subsidies under GATT, "GATT provides little discipline on subsidies that cannot be characterized as export subsidies, instead merely permitting countervailing duties that may further distort trade."[12] And he concludes that cooperation for agreed competition rules at the international level is necessary.

Bernard M. Hoekman and Petros C. Mavroidis suggest the use of another instrument, namely GATT article 23:1(b),[13] which concerns a "nonviolation complaint"; that is, a case in which it is argued that the action is not a violation but has nonetheless nullified or impaired prior negotiated conditions of market access. Passive support, such as exemptions from enforcement—or nonenforcement—of antitrust, may be sufficient to bring complaints before GATT. But Hoekman and Mavroidis also recognize that "the reach of GATT is limited."[14] Among the "lacunae" that are singled out, three are directly connected with competition policy:

— to be attacked as a violation of GATT, private business practices restricting access to markets must be supported by the government;

— competition policy per se is not addressed by GATT; and

— the reach of GATT is restricted to action or inaction by governments that affect the conditions of competition in their markets. GATT does not discipline export cartels or actions by governments themselves that have detrimental effects on competition in export markets.

12. Trachtman (1993, p. 102).
13. Hoekman and Mavroidis (1994, p. 22).
14. Hoekman and Mavroidis (1994, p. 28).

Clearly GATT has a lot to offer, including the judicial system that its dispute resolution mechanism has developed, and can be used more efficiently. But new initiatives in the area of international competition policy, within the framework of the World Trade Organization, are also desirable, especially to ensure a proper enforcement of substantive rules.

In Scherer's proposals this issue of enforcement, narrowly linked with the question of sovereignty, remains tricky. His proposal 7 states that beginning seven years after the creation of an International Competition Policy Office, this institution "will determine whether an abuse exists, and if so, recommend corrective measures. If national authorities fail to take corrective action, the World Trade Organization will authorize appropriate sanctions." But an abuse standard is very ambiguous, and the appropriate sanction is not easily identified, with retaliation generally leading to further distorted trade.

Another approach that questions the relevance of an international competition policy is based on the efficiency of competition between competition policies. "Competition laws are just like cars in that they improve through competition."[15] Such competition could cause governments to produce the best practices and permit a greater respect for diversity and cultural specificity. Conversely, harmonizing is dangerous because there is no agreement yet about the basic functions of antitrust; countries might harmonize to the wrong standard, since they have not determined the "correct" competition policy in many areas. Furthermore, as noted, competition policy cannot be singled out as a topic but must be understood in its relations with other industrial and social policies.

These arguments cannot be totally rejected, and the principles of subsidiarity must be respected, including decentralized implementation. But it is also well known that the market of government policy is imperfect, that a race to the bottom could take place, leading to lax competition policies, and that many restrictive practices involve spillovers across countries that could not be easily internalized by decentralized authorities. Competition among jurisdiction policies could also impede trade and investment and thus be welfare reducing, given the created opacity and insecurity.

Similarly, the danger of a harmonization viewed as a westernization of the rules of the game must be recognized. The role of history in explaining different approaches to competition policy is important. Indeed there are differences in attitudes toward economic power (private and public), freedom of contract and trade, efficiency, and equity that are grounded in dissimilarities in political, cultural, and moral history—what Corwin

15. Meessen (1993, p. 18).

Edwards calls the "cultural inheritance."[16] A well-known illustration is Japan's poor record of punishing antitrust violators: the number of procedures actually launched is low, evidence is difficult to obtain, and penalties are weak.[17] One of the explanations of such a situation lies in the crucial role of consensus in Japanese society.

But as the world economy becomes increasingly globalized, such differences cannot put into question the aim of reconciling domestic practices when they strongly discriminate, directly or indirectly, against foreign firms and products. This view does not require a complete harmonization but corresponds to the concept of "deep integration," according to which the degree of integration required in a globalized economic environment goes beyond the principle of national treatment. As suggested by the EC 1992 exercise, it implies that in areas crucial for international competition, some minimum standards covering several public policies must be adopted in a multilateral, cooperative way. This approach, in the framework of the new World Trade Organization, is probably a first best, but it will also be a long and painful process. A series of "open" bilateral or trilateral initiatives could then be a complementary vehicle for multilateralism, having a domino effect. Such initiatives overcome the difficulty of achieving detailed and forcible agreements on complex matters among a large group of highly disparate nations, and simultaneously they demonstrate the gains for participating rather than being left out. An important example is the U.S.-EC cooperation agreement mentioned by Scherer. This transatlantic agreement could be a model for other countries and merits a specific analysis.

Three aspects can be emphasized. First, the U.S.-EC agreement contains a radical provision: it calls for coordinated *enforcement* activities when such coordination is in the mutual interest of both parties (article 4). Second, if a party believes that anticompetitive activities carried out on the territory of the other party are adversely affecting its important interests, the first party may notify the other one and may request that the other party's competition authorities initiate appropriate enforcement activities (article 5). This "positive" comity is a valuable attempt to deal affirmatively and nonconfrontationally with an alternative to extraterritorial enforcement.[18] Third, a particular concern in the working of

16. Edwards (1967).

17. In the 1990 structural impediments initiative talks, Japan agreed to specify and make clear the practices that are unlawful in its distribution system and within the system of *keiretsu*. In the wake of U.S. criticism, investigative staff of the Fair Trade Commission have been increased and fines have been lifted. From 1985 to 1990 the number of companies penalized for cartel agreements quadrupled, and the total penalties imposed by the Fair Trade Commission increased thirtyfold.

18. See Rill (1993).

the agreement is the question of confidentiality. Establishing a trusting relationship between the parties involved and the regulator is essential; concerns could arise about multinational agencies' not having developed a tradition of confidentiality. Article 8 of the agreement deals with that problem.[19] But as underlined by Rill, the laws of the United States and the European Community already protect the confidentiality of business information in several contexts.[20] For example, the EC strictly limits the extent to which the enforcement agencies can share information, preventing agencies from sharing confidential information obtained as part of pre-merger notification filings.

In the end, the key for securing international consent to a minimum set of common competition policies is mutual trust based on shared values. To obtain such a trust requires a slow, progressive learning process.

19. According to article 8:

(1) Notwithstanding any other provision of this Agreement, neither Party is required to provide information to the other Party if disclosure of that information to the requesting Party (a) is prohibited by the law of the Party possessing the information, or (b) would be incompatible with important interests of the Party possessing the information.

(2) Each Party agrees to maintain, to the fullest extent possible, the confidentiality of any information provided to it in confidence by the other Party under this Agreement and to oppose, to the fullest extent possible, any application for disclosure of such information by a third party that is not authorized by the Party that supplied the information.

20. Rill (1993).

Jiro Tamura

The endeavor to harmonize competition laws, especially antimonopoly laws, among advanced industrialized nations has evolved from the globalization of the world economy and the concern for fairness in international trade. Of specific interest is the decreasing role of the cartel in Japan, as well as efforts to minimize the market- exclusionary effects of Japanese *keiretsu*, a uniquely domestic form of economic organization.

In these comments I elucidate some of the many changes that the organization of the Japanese economy has undergone, primarily the harmonization of Japanese antimonopoly law enforcement with that of other economically mature trading nations. I also explain new trends in Japanese market regulation, in particular the dissolution of cartels, greater efficiency in the distribution system, and a strengthened Fair Trade Commission equipped with legal power and staff to better protect the interests of the Japanese consumer.

These trends appear to be gradually converging with American and European styles of competition-based legal regulation. It is essential to note that both Japanese and American-European systems of market regulation are influenced by legal traditions, different national priorities, and complex social influences. In short, change in these respects in Japan is slow, but it is nevertheless moving in the right direction.

The concern for fairness in international trade has developed, among other reasons, because of the vagueness and ambiguity of "fairness" itself. Here fairness can be interpreted as the ability of enterprises from different countries to compete internationally under similar conditions.[1] In contrast, one effect of a cartel is to deprive competitors of market entry. There are two kinds of cartels in Japan: government-exemption cartels, which are often accompanied by outsider regulation; and private illegal cartels, which are maintained by exclusionary practices. In both cases the interests of the cartel participants are maintained at the expense of the potential competitor. Therefore, cartels are "unfair" if, among other things, they serve as a barrier to market entry.

Jiro Tamura is an associate professor in the Faculty of Policy Management at Keio University.

1. Concern for "fairness" has been a long-standing point of negotiation in U.S.-Japanese relations. Both the structural impediments initiative and the framework talks were attempts to mete out an agreement on fairness in the bilateral trade of goods and services. Furthermore, the 1988 Omnibus Trade and Competitiveness Act (Super 301) enumerates any act or policy "unreasonable" if " it denies fair and equitable" treatment. Technically, this is Section 301 of the Trade Act of 1974, as amended.

Japan has a long history of government-sanctioned cartels.[2] In the late 1960s the number of cartels exempted from antimonopoly law scrutiny was more than 1,000; in 1994 the number was considerably less than 100. With the abolishment of the middle-size fiber companies cartel exemption, the number of officially exempted cartels has further declined.[3] The total number of cartels has also been reduced, and the accompanying outsider regulation laws that served to protect these cartels from international competition have been changed. Despite these changes, domestic firms in many markets have established strong positions, complete with distribution networks and relationships that impede foreign market entry. Therefore, in describing the "unfair" market entry aspects of Japan, the heart of the problem lies in the market structures that developed after years of protection. The solution lies in, among other things, a more stringent application of antimonopoly law.

An important first step in trying to create fair market access for enterprises operating internationally is the convergence and transparency of legal systems. When considering the international harmonization of antitrust law, one finds concepts that can be harmonized with relative ease, whereas others prove more problematic.

The Japanese antimonopoly law is based in many respects on U.S. antitrust law. The main provisions of Japanese antimonopoly law are applicable to the following three categories of conduct: (1) private monopolization, (2) unreasonable restraint of trade, and (3) unfair business practices. An explication of the legal technicalities of these three categories goes beyond the scope of my comments here. It suffices to note that the Fair Trade Commission has the same guiding principle and modus operandi as its American and European market regulatory counterparts.

In 1993 the commission further clarified its strict enforcement efforts by announcing to the other relevant ministries (MITI, MoF, and so forth) and government offices that they should come to an agreement and press for the abolishment of exemptions for cartels.[4] By gaining support to enlarge its range of antimonopoly enforcement and at the same time using the administrative tool of taking cartels away from the other ministries, the commission seeks to strengthen domestic competition policy and its own role in regulating the Japanese economy.

Despite these efforts, the Japanese restriction of cartels may be considered less active compared with American and European efforts, yet the requirements for enforcement are theoretically the same. Hence the

2. It is not the point of these comments to show the effect of cartels, positive, negative, or otherwise, on the economic development of Japan.

3. Terakawa (1994, p. 21).

4. *Nihon Keizei Shinbun* (Nikkei Newspaper), November 2, 1993.

discrepancy in antimonopoly activity is based less on the law itself than on the weakness of the enforcement of the law.

This trend is changing. Largely as a result of the U.S.-Japan Structural Impediments Initiative,[5] the Fair Trade Commission has added staff, increasing the investigative division by almost 40 percent, from 129 to 178 persons. Furthermore, the commission has raised its surcharge on corporations from 1.5 to 6 percent of total sales of a particular product found to be in violation of the law.[6] Besides these structural changes, there is evidence that the commission is preparing to take a new role in prosecution.

Recently the commission has enjoyed increased cooperation with the public prosecutor's office. In the past, because the two offices lacked coordination, the criminal prosecution of antimonopoly law violations was effectively stifled. To solve the problem of jurisdiction, a joint "indictment issue conference" has been created to bring the commission closer to the public prosecutor's office. Along with intensified prosecution, the criminal penalty for offense has been raised from approximately $40,000 to $800,000.[7] It is evident that Japan is gradually heading toward convergence in effecting the integration of competition policies with criminal prosecution to achieve legal results with greater transparency.

Aside from recognizing the basic guiding principle of protecting competition in the marketplace, Japan, the United States, and Europe have similar legal statutes. For example, cartels are generally prohibited by OECD countries[8] and can therefore be considered a point of departure for the harmonization of competition policies.

Vertical restrictions, defined as agreements between vertically related firms in which the "upstream" party, usually the manufacturer, imposes "restrictions on distribution" upon the distributor and retailer, pose another problem to nondomestic enterprises trying to enter another market. To clarify its position on vertical restrictions, the commission released guidelines in July 1991 to ensure active enforcement. The guidelines state:

> It is essential to promote free and fair competition and enable the market mechanism to fully perform its functions: more specifically, to make sure that (1) firms not be prevented from freely entering a market, (2) each firm can freely and independently select its customers or suppliers,

5. The Structural Impediments Initiative was a bilateral working group initiated in 1989 and terminated in 1992. The purpose of the working group was to reduce structural impediments to the bilateral flow of goods and services.

6. See Fair Trade Commission (1992).

7. Fair Trade Commission (1992).

8. OECD (1984, p. 39).

(3) price and other transactions terms can be set via each firm's free and independent business judgement, and (4) competition be engaged in by fair means on the basis of price, quality, and service.[9]

Vertical restraints unprosecuted can have serious effects on a domestic economy. They can effectively deny competitors access to distribution systems and retailers. This problem is especially acute in Japan, owing to various government regulations and the unique form of corporate organization called *keiretsu*, which can have the effect of excluding foreign and domestic competitors because of vertical restraints up and down the distribution stream. The recent revision of the large-scale retail store law (government regulation), which reduces the approximately ten-year administrative waiting period to less than two years for potential market entrants to be permitted to open a large retail store, has allowed more room for competition at the distribution level.[10] In this respect, the antimonopoly law is well developed to bring cases against anticompetitive behavior, primarily under the unfair business practice clause of the antimonopoly law.

The Japanese system of distribution, or *keiretsu*, has been the target of criticism from the United States and EC countries, but now a significant change is occurring as a result of the emergence of discounters at the retail level. In effect, the Japanese distribution system that used to play a role in blocking foreign market entry is collapsing under its own inefficiency. There has been a recent trend in Japan for discount retailing, especially evident in the alcohol, food, cosmetics, clothing, furniture, and even restaurant markets. As consumers' values change and demand continues to grow, the discounters are not just providing merchandise but also guiding new trends in the retail-distribution sector, which has long been protected and regulated.

In the cosmetics market, a small retailer called Fujiki Honten is taking on Shiseido, Japan's largest cosmetics manufacturer. For decades Fujiki has been selling Shiseido products by mail order, at 20 percent discount. Given the Japanese recession and the convenience of having the products sent directly to one's home, Fujiki quickly became popular. Yet cosmetics are primarily sold in Japan by means of "chain store" agreements, which place a network of companies under the one firm, Shiseido. Because of this relationship, Shiseido has complete knowledge of wholesale purchase volume, sales, and stock volume. The purpose of the strict relationship is to maintain price levels and thus make discounting products almost impossible. By 1990 Fujiki had more than 100,000 customers and annual sales of 1.2 billion yen and growing. Suddenly Fujiki's twenty-eight-year-old chain store agreement was canceled. Shiseido's official claim was that Fujiki had

9. Fair Trade Commission (1991, p. 1).
10. Daikibo Kouri Tenpo Ho, Law 109 (law on the adjustment of operations by retail business with respect to large-scale retail stores).

violated the contract that mandates that sales be done face to face, or over the counter, making no mention of the twenty-eight years that Shiseido company officials had urged Fujiki to stop discounting. Simply, if Shiseido gave cut-price sales as the official reason for the termination of contract, it could be found guilty of "resale price control activity."[11]

Despite an apparent violation of the antimonopoly law, the Fair Trade Commission failed to investigate the case. Unsatisfied, Fujiki filed a case against Shiseido at the Tokyo District Court, asking the court to find Shiseido's termination of contract illegal and to compel Shiseido to resume supplying products to Fujiki. The District Court responded that 517,180,000 units of Shiseido products should be sent to Fujiki because there was an illegal termination of contract. The court further stated that "the Shiseido contract chain store system is restricting the sales method and thereby maintaining price without reasonable justification. It is highly possible that it will violate the legal implication of antimonopoly law."[12] Shiseido immediately appealed the ruling to the Tokyo High Court, and while the case is pending, Fujiki cannot obtain Shiseido products.

In response to its failure to fully investigate Fujiki's claim, the commission has recently started to fully investigate the claim of another Shiseido discounter, Kawachiya, which also suffered an abrupt termination of contract. Fujiki and Kawachiya together have formed a new organization, the Association of Cosmetics Discounters, to fight the big cosmetic makers' illegal price controls.

In Japan the cosmetics market is very large but has been dominated by a few large firms. The ability of those firms to eliminate price competition created a distribution system that was rigid and basically impenetrable to both foreign and domestic competitors. Yet with increasing instances of free competition in the market, compounded by the recession, Japanese consumers' awareness of price competition in the form of discounts has increased. The discount stores, with the support of consumers, have gained power in acting against the manufacturers' trying to control distribution. In the end, increased Japanese consumer demand for lower prices and greater distribution efficiency will lead to greater competition.

Competition, if properly protected by the commission, will lead to increasing market entry opportunities for both foreign and domestic competitors.

Overall, Japan has strengthened and is continuing to strengthen its enforcement of antimonopoly law while at the same time attempting to

11. "Unfair Business Practices," General Designation 12, under article 19 of the antimonoply law.
12. Tokyo District Court, Case 15347, September 27, 1993.

remove barriers to market entry into Japan. In the long run these efforts should help diffuse tension between Japan and its major trading partners. Most important, the thrust for legal transparency in the competition policy arena has had an educational effect on the participants within the Japanese market, especially the consumer.

As for the international harmonization of antitrust policy, there have been many positive global trends. For example, the United States has formalized its commitment to improved mutual antitrust understanding by entering into bilateral cooperative agreements with Canada, the European Community, and Australia. The U.S. agreement with the EC, signed in September 1991, has unusual features that could help shape the future of bilateral extraterritorial competition policy agreements.[13] In general, bilateral antimonopoly agreements are becoming increasingly common, and the commission has been meeting annually with analogous enforcement officials from the United States and the European Community. These bilateral talks strengthen the cooperative economic system's ability to resolve issues arising from regulatory spillover effects and avoid international conflicts over antimonopoly application. In this respect, bilateral antitrust enforcement agreements are a useful tool in minimizing the need for such international trade policy as Super 301, which is unilateral.[14]

As regards competition policy, Japan is not necessarily the outlier that many businessmen and scholars perceive it to be. Moreover, several avenues exist for solving problems if exclusionary practices persist. First, America and Europe should continue to request that the Fair Trade Commission enforce the antimonopoly law against specific anticompetitive practices. Second, both bilateral and multilateral systems of international cooperation, through a treaty or memorandum of understanding, should be created to formalize the process of transnational antitrust notification and consultation.

If these initial efforts fail to yield results, the extraterritorial application of antitrust law within the confines of international comity can be considered as a final option to maintain free and fair international trade. It is important to emphasize that extraterritorial application of domestic antitrust law must be a solution of last resort so as to place a priority on promoting cohesive and converging competition policies in an increasingly international market.

13. The agreement provides that the principal enforcement agencies of both countries coordinate their respective enforcement activities when any anticompetitive activity harms the interests of both countries. Also, the agreement empowers one party with the right to request an investigation of an alleged anticompetitive practice consummated on the other's soil.

14. Super 301 is designed to combat trade practices that restrict U.S. foreign market access. In doing so, it requires the U.S. trade representative to pursue designated unfair trade practices of "priority nations" that have "barriers" or "trade distorting practices."

References

American Bar Association. 1991. *Report of the ABA Section of Antitrust Law Special Committee on International Antitrust.* Chicago.

Amsden, Alice H. 1989. *Asia's Next Giant: South Korea and Late Industrialization.* Oxford University Press.

Andewelt, Roger B. 1984. "Analysis of Patent Pools under the Antitrust Law." *Antitrust Law Journal* 53(3): 611–40.

Areeda, Philip, and Donald F. Turner. 1976. "Scherer on Predatory Pricing: A Reply." *Harvard Law Review* 89 (March): 891–900.

Audretsch, David B. 1989. "Legalized Cartels in West Germany." *Antitrust Bulletin* 34 (Fall): 579–600.

Baer, Herbert L. 1984. "Competition among the Multinationals: An Examination of Equilibrium in Multimarket Oligopolies." Ph.D. dissertation, Northwestern University.

Ball, Sir James. 1993. "The World Economy: Trends and Prospects for the Next Decade." Report to the British–North American Committee. December.

Baur, Jürgen F. 1980. "The Control of Mergers between Large, Financially Strong Firms in West Germany." *Zeitschrift für die gesamte Staatswissenschaft* 136 (September): 444–64.

Berge, Wendell. 1944. *Cartels: Challenge to a Free World.* Washington: Public Affairs Press.

Bezirganian, Steve D. 1993. "U.S. Affiliates of Foreign Companies: Operations in 1991." *Survey of Current Business* 73 (May): 89–99.

Bhagwati, Jagdish, and Hugh T. Patrick, eds. 1990. *Aggressive Unilateralism: America's 301 Trade Policy and the World Trading System.* University of Michigan Press.

Bisson, Thomas A. 1954. *Zaibatsu Dissolution in Japan.* University of California Press.

Blaich, Fritz. 1970. "Der 'Standard-Oil-Fall' vor dem Reichstag." *Zeitschrift für die gesamte Staatswissenschaft* 126 (October): 663–82.

———. 1974. "Robert Liefmann und das Problem der staatlichen Kartellpolitik." *Jahrbuch für Sozialwissenschaft* 25(1): 138–57.

Blakeney, Michael, and Fiona Patfield. 1991. "Australia." In *Competition Laws of the Pacific Rim Countries,* edited by Julian von Kalinowski. New York: Matthew Bender.

Bloch, Kurt. 1932. "On German Cartels." *Journal of Business of the University of Chicago* 5 (July): 213–22.

Boner, Roger Alan, and Reinald Krueger. 1991. *The Basics of Antitrust Policy: A Review of Ten Nations and the European Communities.* World Bank Technical Paper 160. Washington: World Bank.

Bork, Robert H. 1966. "Legislative Intent and the Policy of the Sherman Act." *Journal of Law and Economics* 9 (October): 7–48.

Boserup, William, and Uffe Schlichtkrull. 1962. "Alternative Approaches to the Control of Competition." In *Competition Cartels and Their Regulation: An Outline of European Cartel Legislation and its Administration,* edited by John Perry Miller, 59–113. Amsterdam: North-Holland.

Bourdet, Yves. 1988. *International Integration, Market Structure, and Prices.* London: Routledge.

Bourgeois, Jacques H. J. 1993. "Competition Policy and Commercial Policy." In *The European Community's Commercial Policy after 1992: The Legal Dimension,* edited by Marc Maresceau, 113–33. Boston: Martinus Nijhoff.

Bowman, Ward S., Jr. 1973. *Patent and Antitrust Law: A Legal and Economic Appraisal.* University of Chicago Press.

Brandeis, Louis D. 1914. *Other People's Money and How the Bankers Use It.* New York: Stokes.

Brittan, Sir Leon. 1992. "A Framework for International Competition." Address before the World Economic Forum. Davos, Switzerland, February 3.

———. 1992. "Making a Reality of the Single Market: Pharmaceutical Pricing." Speech before the IEA Health and Welfare Unit. London, December 1.

Bullock, Charles J. 1901. "Trust Literature: A Survey and a Criticism." *Quarterly Journal of Economics* 15 (February). Reprinted in Scherer (1993, vol. 2, pp. 5–55).

Caves, Richard E. 1980. "Productivity Differences among Industries." In *Britain's Economic Performance,* edited by Richard E. Caves and Lawrence B. Krause, 135–98. Brookings.

———. 1982. *Multinational Enterprise and Economic Analysis.* Cambridge University Press.

———.1987. "Industrial Policy and Trade Policy: The Connections." In *Protection and Competition in International Trade,* edited by Henryk Kierhowski, 68–85. Oxford: Basil Blackwell.

Chandler, Alfred D., Jr. 1990. *Scale and Scope: The Dynamics of Industrial Capitalism.* Cambridge, Mass.: Belknap Press.

"Collaboration, Innovation and Antitrust." 1990. *Journal of Economic Perspectives* 4 (Summer): 75–130.

Commission of the European Communities. 1972. *First Report on Competition Policy.* Brussels. April.

Cowling, Keith, and others. 1980. *Mergers and Economic Performance.* Cambridge University Press.

d'Aspremont, Claude, and Alexis Jacquemin. 1988. "Cooperative and Non-Cooperative R&D in Duopoly with Spillovers." *American Economic Review* 78 (December): 1133–37.

Davidow, Joel. 1983. "Cartels, Competition Laws and the Regulation of International Trade." *New York University Journal of International Law and Politics* 15 (Winter): 358–89.

Dick, Andrew R. 1991. "Learning by Doing and Dumping in the Semiconductor Industry." *Journal of Law and Economics* 34 (April): 133–60.

"Die Ordnung oder Freiheit." 1993. *Zeit Punkte,* Nr. 3/1993 (*Zeit Magazin,* Hamburg), pp. 74–76.

Dunlop, Bruce, David McQueen, and Michael Trebilcock. 1987. *Canadian Competition Policy: A Legal and Economic Analysis.* Toronto: Canadian Law Book, Inc.

Edwards, Corwin D. 1955. "Conglomerate Bigness as a Source of Power." In *Business Concentration and Price Policy: A Conference of the Universities—National Committee for Economic Research,* 331–52. Princeton University Press.

———. 1964. *Cartelization in Western Europe.* U.S. Department of State, Bureau of Intelligence and Research.

———. 1967. *Control of Cartels and Monopolies: An International Comparison.* Dobbs Ferry, N.Y.: Oceana Publications.

Fair Trade Commission [Japan]. Executive Office. 1991. "The Antimonopoly Act Guidelines Concerning Distribution Systems and Business Practices." Tokyo (July).

———. 1992. "Antimonopoly Law's Strengthening of Deterrence Power and Ensuring of Transparency." Tokyo (March).

Fair Trade Commission [Japan]. Staff Office. 1973. "The Antimonopoly Act of Japan." Tokyo.

Federal Trade Commission. Bureau of Economics. 1967. *Webb-Pomerene Associations: A 50-Year Review.* Washington.

———. 1981. *Statistical Report: Annual Line of Business Report, 1975.* Washington.

———. 1985. *Statistical Report: Annual Line of Business Report, 1977.* Washington.

Flamm, Kenneth. Forthcoming. *Mismanaged Trade? Strategic Policy and the Semiconductor Industry.* Brookings.

Fox, Eleanor M. 1986. "Monopolization and Dominance in the United States and the European Community: Efficiency, Opportunity, and Fairness." *Notre Dame Law Review* 61(5): 990–1004.

———. 1992. "Merger Control in the EEC—Towards a European Merger Jurisprudence." In *1991 Fordham Corporate Law Institute,* edited by B. Hawk, 709–49. New York: Matthew Bender.

Fransman, Martin. 1990. *The Market and Beyond: Cooperation and Competitition in Information Technology Development in the Japanese System.* Cambridge University Press.

Freeman, Christopher. 1987. *Technology Policy and Economic Performance: Lessons from Japan.* London: Pinter.

GATT Secretariat. 1993. *Final Act Embodying the Results of the Uruguay Round of Multilateral Trade Negotiations.* Geneva, December 15.

"General Agreement on Tariffs and Trade." 1947. *United States Treaties and Other International Acts*. Series 1700. U.S. Department of State.

George, Ken. 1990. "UK Competition Policy: Issues and Institutions." In *Competition Policy in Europe and North America: Economic Issues and Institutions*, edited by W. S. Comanor and others, 104–45. New York: Harwood Academic.

George, Ken, and Alexis Jacquemin. 1990. "Competition Policy in the European Community." In *Competition Policy in Europe and North America: Economic Issues and Institutions*, edited by W. S. Comanor and others, 206–45. New York: Harwood Academic.

Hadley, Arthur T. 1887. "Private Monopolies and Public Rights." *Quarterly Journal of Economics* 1 (October). Reprinted in Scherer (1993, vol. 1, pp. 30–46).

Hamburger, Richard A. 1962. "Coal and Steel Community: Rules for a Competitive Market and Their Applications." In *Competition Cartels and Their Regulation: An Outline of European Cartel Legislation and its Administration*, edited by John Perry Miller, 347–71. Amsterdam: North-Holland.

Hamilton, Alexander. 1791. "Report on the Subject of Manufactures." In *The Papers of Alexander Hamilton, vol. 10: December 1791–January 1792*, edited by Harold C. Syrett, 266–91. Columbia University Press, 1966.

Hatfield, Henry R. 1899. "The Chicago Trust Conference." *Journal of Political Economy* 8 (December): 1–18.

Hawley, Ellis W. 1966. *The New Deal and the Problem of Monopoly: A Study in Economic Ambivalence*. Princeton University Press.

Hay, Donald, and John Vickers. 1988. "The Reform of UK Competition Policy." *National Institute Economic Review* (August): 56–68.

Hazlett, Thomas W. 1992. "The Legislative History of the Sherman Act Re-examined." *Economic Inquiry* 30 (April): 263–76.

Hicks, John R. 1935. "Annual Survey of Economic Theory: The Theory of Monopoly." *Econometrica* 3 (January): 1–20.

Hjalmarsson, Lennart. 1992. "Competition Policy and Economic Efficiency: Efficiency Trade-offs in Industrial Policy. In *Internationalization, Market Power and Consumer Welfare*, edited by Yves Bourdet, 337–43. London: Routledge.

Hoekman, Bernard M., and Petros C. Mavroidis. 1994. "Competition, Competition Policy and the GATT." Discussion Paper 876. London: Centre for Economic Policy Research.

Hurwitz, James D., and William E. Kovacic. 1982. "Judicial Analysis of Predation: The Emerging Trends." *Vanderbilt Law Review* 35 (January): 63–157.

Imamura, S. 1973. "Consumer and Competition Policy." In *International Conference on International Economy and Competition Policy*, edited by M. Ariga, 289–92. Tokyo: Japanese Institute of Business Law.

Institute for International Legal Information. 1992. *"The Dunkel Draft" from the GATT Secretariat*. Buffalo: Hein.

Iyori, Hiroshi, and Akinori Uesugi. 1983. *The Antimonoply Laws of Japan*. Quoted in *Competing about Competition*, by Carl Martin Wolfrum. Koblenz, Germany: Praxisarbeit, Wissenschaftliche Hochschule für Unternemensführung Koblenz, 1991.

Jacquemin, Alexis. 1990. "Horizontal Concentration and European Merger Policy." *European Economic Review* 34 (May): 539–50.

Jacquemin, Alexis, Pierre Buigues, and Fabienne Ilzkovitz. 1989. "Horizontal Mergers and Competition Policy in the European Community." *European Economy* 40 (May): 68–69.

Jacquemin, Alexis, and others. 1981. "A Dynamic Analysis of Export Cartels: The Japanese Case." *Economic Journal* 91 (September): 685–96.

"Japanese Fair Trade Commission Decision on the Yawata-Fuji Steel Merger." 1970. *Antitrust Bulletin* 15 (Winter): 803–27.

Jenny, Frederic. 1990. "French Competition Policy in Perspective." In *Competition Policy in Europe and North America: Economic Issues and Institutions,* edited by W. S. Comanor and others, 146–88. New York: Harwood Academic.

———. 1991. "Merger Control in France." In *International Mergers and Joint Ventures,* Proceedings of the Fordham Corporate Law Institute. Ardsley-on-Hudson, N.Y.: Transnational Juris Publications.

———. 1992. "EEC Merger Control: Economies as an Antitrust Defence or an Antitrust Attack?" Paper presented at the Fordham Corporate Law Institute on EC and U.S. Competition Law and Policy. October.

Johnson, Harry G. 1965. "Optimal Trade Intervention in the Presence of Domestic Distortions." In *Trade, Growth, and the Balance of Payments,* edited by Robert E. Baldwin and others, 3–34. Chicago: Rand McNally.

Kalt, Joseph P. 1988. "The Political Economy of Protectionism: Tariffs and Retaliation in the Timber Industry." In *Trade Policy Issues and Empirical Analysis,* edited by Robert E. Baldwin, 339–68. University of Chicago Press.

Kaplow, Louis. 1984. "The Patent-Antitrust Intersection." *Harvard Law Review* 97 (June): 1813–92.

Katz, Michael L. 1986. "An Analysis of Cooperative Research and Development." *Rand Journal of Economics* 17 (Winter): 527–43.

Kaufer, Erich. 1980. "The Control of the Abuse of Market Power by Market-Dominating Companies under the German Law against Restraints of Competition." *Zeitschrift für die gesamte Staatswissenschaft* 136 (September): 510–32.

Kennedy, Paul M. 1987. *The Rise and Fall of the Great Powers: Economic Change and the Military Conflict from 1500 to 2000.* Random House.

Keynes, John Maynard. 1936. *The General Theory of Employment Interest and Money.* Harcourt, Brace.

Klein, Burton H. 1977. *Dynamic Economics.* Harvard University Press.

Knickerbocker, Frederick T. 1973. *Oligopolistic Reaction and Multinational Enterprise.* Harvard University, Graduate School of Business Administration.

Komiya, Ryutaro. 1990. *The Japanese Economy: Trade, Industry, and Government.* Tokyo University Press. Reprinted in Scherer (1993, vol. 1, pp. 190–95).

Kreps, David M., and Robert Wilson. 1982. "Reputation and Imperfect Information." *Journal of Economic Theory* 27 (August): 253–79.

Krugman, Paul R., ed. 1986. *Strategic Trade Policy and the New International Economics.* MIT Press.

———. 1990. *Rethinking International Trade.* MIT Press.

Lande, Robert H. 1982. "Wealth Transfers as the Original and Primary Concern of Antitrust." *Hastings Law Journal* 34 (September): 65–151.

Lawrence, Robert Z. 1991. "Efficient or Exclusionist? The Import Behavior of Japanese Corporate Groups." *Brookings Papers on Economic Activity* 1: 311–30.

Lawrence, Robert Z., and Charles L. Schultze, eds. 1990. *An American Trade Strategy: Options for the 1990s.* Brookings.

Letwin, William. 1965. *Law and Economic Policy in America: The Evolution of the Sherman Antitrust Act.* Random House.

Levin, Richard C., and others. 1987. "Appropriating the Returns from Industrial Research and Development." *Brookings Papers on Economic Activity* 3: 783–820.

List, Friedrich. [1841] 1916. *The National System of Political Economy,* translated by Sampson S. Lloyd. London: Longmans, Green.

Lockwood, William W. 1968. *The Economic Development of Japan: Growth and Structural Change.* Princeton University Press.

Mackay, Robert J., James C. Miller III, and Bruce Yandle, eds. 1987. *Public Choice and Regulation: A View from Inside the Federal Trade Commission.* Stanford: Hoover Institution Press.

Mann, Charles C., and Mark L. Plummer. 1991. *The Aspirin Wars: Money, Medicine, and 100 Years of Rampant Competition.* Harvard Business School Press.

Mansfield, Edwin. 1986. "Patents and Innovation: An Empirical Study." *Management Science* 32 (February): 173–81.

Marshall, Alfred. 1961. *Principles of Economics,* 9th ed. (variorum), vol. 1, edited and annotated by C. W. Guillebaud. London: Macmillan.

Mason, Edward S. 1946. *Controlling World Trade: Cartels and Commodity Agreements.* McGraw-Hill.

Mataloni, Raymond J., Jr. 1992. "U.S. Multinational Companies: Operations in 1990." *Survey of Current Business* 72 (August): 60–69.

Matsushita, Mitsuo. 1986. "An International Comparison of Distribution and Trade Practices and Competition Policies." Draft report of an International Comparative Study Group on Distribution Structures and Trade Practices. Tokyo. April.

Meeks, Geoffrey. 1977. *Disappointing Marriage: A Study of the Gains from Merger.* Cambridge University Press.

Meessen, Karl M. 1989. "Competition of Competition Laws." *Northwestern Journal of International Law and Business* 10 (Spring): 17–30.

"Merger Regulation in the United Kingdom" 1990. *International Merger Law: Events and Commentary* 1 (September): 16.

Merrill Lynch Business Brokerage and Valuation. 1993. *Mergerstat Review, 1992.* Schaumburg, Illinois.

Messerlin, Patrick A. 1989a. "Antidumping Regulations or Protrust Law? The EC Chemical Cases." Washington: World Bank.

———. 1989b. "The EC Antidumping Regulations: A First Economic Appraisal, 1980–85." *Weltwirtschaftliches Archiv* 125(3): 563–87.

Mestmäcker, Ernst-Joachim. 1980. "Competition Policy and Antitrust: Some Comparative Observations." *Zeitschrift für die gesamte Staatswissenschaft* 136 (September): 386–404.

Milgrom, Paul, and John Roberts. 1982. "Predation, Reputation, and Entry Deterrence." *Journal of Economic Theory* 27 (August): 280–312.

Millon, David. 1990. "The First Antitrust Statute." *Washburn Law Journal* 29 (Winter): 141–49.

Mirow, Kurt Rudolf, and Harry Maurer. 1982. *Webs of Power: International Cartels and the World Economy.* Houghton Mifflin.

Mitchell, Edward J., ed. 1979. *Oil Pipelines and Public Policy: An Analysis of Proposals for Industry Reform and Reorganization.* Washington: American Enterprise Institute.

Murray, Tracy. 1991. "The Administration of the Antidumping Duty Law by the Department of Commerce." In *Down in the Dumps: Administration of the Unfair Trade Laws*, edited by Richard Boltuck and Robert E. Litan, 23–63. Brookings.

National Science Board. 1992. *Science and Engineering Indicators, 1991*, 10th ed. Washington: National Science Foundation.

Nelson, Richard R. 1961. "Uncertainty, Learning, and the Economics of Parallel Research and Development Efforts." *Review of Economics and Statistics* 43 (November): 351–68.

Niederleithinger, Ernst. 1985. "Gesetz gegen Wettbewerbs beschränkungen: Freiheitsschutz oder Wirtschaftsverwaltung?" *Wirtschaft und Wettbewerb* 1: 5–17.

Niino, Kojiro. 1962. "The Logic of Excessive Competition—with Reference to the Japanese Inter-Firm Competition." *Kobe University Economic Review* 8. Reprinted in Scherer (1993, vol. 1, pp. 178–89).

Organization for Economic Cooperation and Development (OECD). 1984. *Competition and Trade Policies: Their Interaction.* Paris.

———. 1986. *The OECD Guidelines for Multinational Enterprises.* Paris.

———. 1987. *Competition Policy in OECD Countries, 1984–1985.* Paris.

———. 1989a. *Competition Policy in OECD Countries, 1987–1988.* Paris.

———. 1989b. *Predatory Pricing.* Paris.

———. 1992a. *Competition Policy in OECD Countries, 1989–1990.* Paris.

———. 1992b. *Historical Statistics, 1960–1990.* Paris.

———. 1993a. *Competition Policy in OECD Countries, 1990–1991.* Paris.

———. 1993b. *Obstacles to Trade and Competition.* Paris.

Peck, M. J., Richard C. Levin, and Akira Goto. 1988. "Picking Losers: Public Policy toward Declining Industries in Japan." In *Government Policy towards Industry in the United States and Japan*, edited by John B. Shoven, 224–25. Cambridge University Press.

Rabinowitz, Mitchell. 1993. "Single Country Export Cartels: Antitrust Law and Policy Options." Harvard Law School, term paper.

Report of the Attorney General's National Committee to Study the Antitrust Laws. 1955. March.

Restrictive Trade Practices Commission. 1986. "Report on Competition in the Canadian Petroleum Industry: Summary." June 16.

Rhoades, Stephen A., and Arnold Heggestad. 1985. "Multimarket Interdependence and Performance in Banking: Two Tests." *Antitrust Bulletin* 30 (Winter): 975–95.

Rill, James F. 1993. "Global Convergence of Competition Policy: The US-EC Competition Agreements." *The Forum of US-EC Legal-Economic Affairs.* Mentor Group. September.

Roosevelt, The Works of Theodore. 1925. vol. 19. Scribners.

Schelling, Thomas C. 1960. *The Strategy of Conflict.* Harvard University Press.

Scherer, F. M. 1966. "Time-Cost Tradeoffs in Uncertain Empirical Research Projects." *Naval Research Logistics Quarterly* 13 (March): 71–82.

———. 1976. "Predatory Pricing and the Sherman Act: A Comment." *Harvard Law Review* 89 (March): 869–890.

———. 1977. *The Economic Effects of Compulsory Patent Licensing.* New York University, Graduate School of Business Administration.

———. 1980. *Industrial Market Structure and Economic Performance,* 2d ed. Houghton Mifflin.

———. 1990a. "Efficiency, Fairness, and the Early Contributions of Economists to the Antitrust Debate." *Washburn Law Journal* 29 (Winter): 243–55.

———. 1990b. "Sunlight and Sunset at the Federal Trade Commission." *Administrative Law Review* 42 (Fall): 461–88.

———. 1992. *International High-Technology Competition.* Harvard University Press.

———, ed. 1993. *Monopoly and Competition Policy.* Hants, U.K.: Edward Elgar.

Scherer, F. M., and Richard S. Belous. 1994. *Unfinished Tasks: The New International Trade Theory and Post-Uruguay Round Challenges.* Washington: British-North American Committee.

Scherer, F. M., and David Ross. 1990. *Industrial Market Structure and Economic Performance,* 3d ed. Houghton Mifflin.

Scherer, F. M., and others. 1975. *The Economics of Multi-Plant Operation: An International Comparisons Study.* Harvard University Press.

Schmidt, Ingo. 1983. "Different Approaches and Problems in Dealing with Control of Market Power: A Comparison of German, European, and U.S. Policy towards Market-Dominating Enterprises." *Antitrust Bulletin* 28 (Summer): 417–60.

———. 1991. "The New EEC Merger Control System." *Review of Industrial Organization* 6(1): 147–59.

———. 1992. "First Experiences with the EEC Merger Control System." In *Competition Policy in an Interdependent World Economy,* edited by Erhard Kantzenbach, Hans-Eckart Scharrer, and Leonard Waverman. Baden-Baden: Nomos Verlagsgesellschaft.

Schmidt, Ingo, and Sabine Richard. 1992. "Conflicts between Antidumping and Antitrust Law in the EC." *Intereconomics* 27 (September-October).

Schwartzman, David. 1993. *The Japanese Television Cartel: A Study Based on Matsushita v. Zenith.* University of Michigan Press.

Scott, John T. 1993. *Purposive Diversification and Economic Performance.* Cambridge University Press.

Servan-Schreiber, J.-J. 1968. *The American Challenge,* translated by Ronald Steel. New York: Atheneum.

Shaw, R. W., and S. A. Shaw. 1983. "Excess Capacity and Rationalisation in the West European Synthetic Fibers Industry." *Journal of Industrial Economics* 32 (December): 149–66.

Shubik, Martin. 1982. *Game Theory in the Social Sciences: Concepts and Solutions.* MIT Press.

Smith, Adam. [1776] 1937. *An Inquiry into the Nature and Causes of the Wealth of Nations.* Modern Library ed. Random House.

The State of Competition in the Canadian Petroleum Industry. 1981. Vol. 1. Ottawa: Bureau of Competition Policy.

Stegemann, Klaus. 1968. "The Functions of Basing Point Pricing and Article 60 of the E.C.S.C. Treaty." *Antitrust Bulletin* 13 (Summer): 411–21.

———. 1977. *Price Competition and Output Adjustment in the European Steel Market.* Tübingen, Germany: Mohr.

———. 1979. "The European Experience with Exempting Specialization Agreements and Recent Proposals to Amend the Combines Investigation Act." In *Canadian Competition Policy: Essays in Law and Economics,* edited by J. Robert S. Prichard and others, 449–86. Toronto: Butterworths.

Stigler, George J. 1982. "The Economists and the Problem of Monopoly." *American Economic Review* 72 (May *Papers and Proceedings, 1981*): 1–11.

Stocking, George W., and Myron W. Watkins. 1946. *Cartels in Action: Case Studies in International Business Diplomacy.* New York: Twentieth Century Fund.

———. 1948. *Cartels or Competition?* New York: Twentieth Century Fund.

Stolper, Gustav, Karl Häuser, and Knut Borchardt. 1967. *The German Economy: 1870 to the Present,* translated by Toni Stolper. Harcourt, Brace and World.

Swann, D. 1970. *The Economics of the Common Market.* Hammondsworth, U.K.: Penguin.

Swann, Dennis, and others. 1974. *Competition in British Industry: Restrictive Practices Legislation in Theory and Practice.* London: Allen and Unwin.

Tarbell, Ida M. 1925. *The Life of Elbert H. Gary: The Story of Steel.* New York: Appleton.

Taussig, Frank W. 1900. "The Iron Industry in the United States." *Quarterly Journal of Economics* 14 (August): 479–804.

Terakawa, Y. 1994. "The Review of the Antimonopoly Law Exemption System" [in Japanese]. *Kousei Torihiki* [Fair Trade] 520 (February).

Thorelli, Hans B. 1954. *The Federal Antitrust Policy: Origination of an American Tradition.* Stockholm: P. A. Norstedt.

Timberg, Sigmund. 1973. "An International Antitrust Convention: A Proposal to Harmonize Conflicting National Policies towards the Multi-National Corporation." *Journal of International Law and Economics* 8 (December): 157–84.

Tirole, Jean. 1988. *The Theory of Industrial Organization.* MIT Press.

Trachtman, Joel. 1993. "International Regulatory Competition, Externalization, and Jurisdiction." *Harvard International Law Journal* 34 (Winter): 47–104.

U.K. Monopolies Commission. 1966. *The British Motor Corporation Ltd. and the Pressed Steel Company Ltd.: A Report on the Merger.* London (January).

United Nations. Transnational Corporations and Management Division, Department of Economics and Social Development. 1992. *World Investment Report 1992: Transnational Corporations as Engines of Growth.* New York.

U.S. Department of Commerce. Bureau of the Census. 1960. *Historical Statistics of the United States: Colonial Times to 1957.* Washington.

U.S. Department of Justice. Antitrust Division. 1982. "Merger Guidelines." June 14.

———. 1984. "Merger Guidelines." June 14.

U.S. Department of State. 1948. *Havana Charter for an International Trade Organization, March 24, 1948.*

U.S. Senate. 1992. *The International Fair Competition Act of 1992.* Report 102–403. 102d Cong. 2d sess. Government Printing Office.

———. Committee on Foreign Relations. 1975. *Multinational Corporations and United States Foreign Policy.* Report of the Subcommittee on Multinational Corporations. 93d Cong. 2 sess. Government Printing Office.

———. Committee on the Judiciary. 1963. *Antitrust Developments in the European Common Market.* Hearings before the Subcommittee on Antitrust and Monopoly. 88 Cong. 1 sess. Government Printing Office.

Victor, A. Paul. 1983. "Antidumping and Antitrust: Can the Inconsistencies Be Resolved?" *New York University Journal of International Law and Politics* 15 (Winter): 339–44.

Vives, Xavier. 1984. "Duopoly Information Equilibrium: Cournot and Bertrand." *Journal of Economic Theory* 34 (October): 71–94.

Voigt, Fritz. 1962. "German Experience with Cartels and Their Control during the Pre-War and Post-War Periods." In *Competition Cartels and Their Regulation,* edited by John Perry Miller, 170–74. Amsterdam: North-Holland.

Waverman, Leonard. 1990. "Canadian Competition Law: 100 Years of Experimentation." In *Competition Policy in Europe and North America: Economic Issues and Institutions,* edited by W. S. Comanor and others, 73–103. New York: Harwood Academic.

———. 1993. "Competition Policy in a Globalized World: Conflicts across Borders." In *Europe and Global Independence,* edited by Leonce Bekemans and Loukas Tsoukalis. Bruges: College of Europe.

Whitney, Simon N. 1958. *Antitrust Policies: American Experience in Twenty Industries.* New York: Twentieth Century Fund.

Wilkins, Mira. 1970. *The Emergence of Multinational Enterprise: American Business Abroad from the Colonial Era to 1914.* Harvard University Press.

Wolfrum, Carl Martin. 1991. *Competing about Competition.* Koblenz, Germany: Praxisarbeit, Wissenschaftliche Hochschule für Unternemensführung Koblenz.

Yergin, Daniel. 1991. *The Prize: The Epic Quest for Oil, Money, and Power.* Simon and Schuster.

Zerbe, Richard. 1969. "The American Sugar Refinery Company, 1887–1914: The Story of a Monopoly." *Journal of Law and Economics* 12 (October): 339–75.

Index